the highest education

becoming a godly man

Gregg Matte

LifeWay Christian Resources
Nashville, Tennessee

Produced by:
National Collegiate Ministry
LifeWay Christian Resources
127 Ninth Avenue North
Nashville, TN 37234
Customer Service: (800) 458-2772

Order additional copies of this book by writing to Customer Service Center, MSN 113;
127 Ninth Avenue, North; Nashville, TN 37234-0153; by calling toll free (800) 458-2772;
by faxing (615) 251-5933; by ordering online at www.lifeway.com;
by emailing customerservice@lifeway.com; or by visiting a LifeWay Christian Store.

For additional information about collegiate ministry resources, training, and events,
visit our Web site at www.crossseekers.org.

Editor: Art Herron
Production Specialist: Leanne Lawrence
Art Director: Ed Crawford

Dewey Decimal Classification: 248.832
Subject Heading: CHRISTIAN LIFE \ SINGLE MEN \ COLLEGE STUDENTS

Unless otherwise noted, Scripture quotations are from the HOLY BIBLE, NEW INTERNATIONAL VERSION.
Copyright © 1973, 1978, 1984 International Bible Society.

ISBN 0-6330-0457-X

LifeWay.

127 Ninth Avenue, North
Nashville, Tennessee 37234-0151

As God works through us, we will help people and churches know Jesus Christ and seek His kingdom
by providing biblical solutions that spiritually transform individuals and cultures.

contents

about the writer

about the writer

Gregg Matte is the director and founder of Breakaway Ministries at Texas A&M University. A nationwide retreat and conference speaker, Gregg graduated from Texas A&M in 1992 and received his master's from Southwestern Seminary in 1999. He lives in Bryan, Texas with his wife Kelly. The foundation of his ministry is his relationship with Jesus Christ: "My call is to follow Christ. Ministry is an overflow of my walk."

The person who inspires me to be a godly man and to whom I am always grateful. Without his contribution, this book would not be published.

Jason Marshall is an assistant baseball coach at McMurry University. After graduating from Texas A&M University in 1992, Jason played four years of professional baseball in the Kansas City Royals organization. He returned to Texas A&M as a student coach before moving to Abilene, Texas, in 1997. Jason sponsors the Fellowship of Christian Athletes at McMurry and has been a guest speaker for church youth and college events, FCA meetings, athletic teams, and summer camps. He and his wife Ashleigh live in Abilene.

The CrossSeekers® Covenant

"You will seek me and find me when you seek me with all your heart." Jeremiah 29:13

As a seeker of the cross of Christ, I am called to break away from trite, nonchalant, laissez-faire Christian living. I accept the challenge to divine daring, to consecrated recklessness for Christ, to devout adventure in the face of ridiculing contemporaries. Created in the image of God and committed to excellence as a disciple of Jesus Christ,

I will seek to be a person of integrity

"Do your best to present yourself to God as one approved, a workman who does not need to be ashamed and who correctly handles the word of truth." 2 Timothy 2:15

My attitudes and actions reveal my commitment to live the kind of life Christ modeled for me—to speak the truth in love, to stand firm in my convictions, to be honest and trustworthy.

I will seek to pursue consistent spiritual growth

"So then, just as you received Christ Jesus as Lord, continue to live in him, rooted and built up in him, strengthened in the faith as you were taught, and overflowing with thankfulness." Colossians 2:6-7

The Christian life is a continuing journey, and I am committed to a consistent, personal relationship with Jesus Christ, to faithful study of His Word, and to regular corporate spiritual growth through the ministry of the New Testament church.

I will seek to speak and live a relevant, authentic, and consistent witness

"Always be prepared to give an answer to everyone who asks you to give the reason for the hope that you have." 1 Peter 3:15

I will tell others the story of how Jesus changed my life, and I will seek to live a radically changed life each day. I will share the good news of Jesus Christ with courage and boldness.

I will seek opportunities to serve in Christ's name

"The Spirit of the Lord is on me, because he has anointed me to preach good news to the poor. He has sent me to proclaim freedom for the prisoners and recovery of sight for the blind, to release the oppressed, to proclaim the year of the Lord's favor." Luke 4:18-19

I believe that God desires to draw all people into a loving, redeeming relationship with Him. As His disciple, I will give myself to be His hands to reach others in ministry and missions.

I will seek to honor my body as the temple of God, dedicated to a lifestyle of purity

"Do you not know that your body is a temple of the Holy Spirit, who is in you, whom you have received from God? You are not your own; you were bought at a price. Therefore honor God with your body." 1 Corinthians 6:19-20

Following the example of Christ, I will keep my body healthy and strong, avoiding temptations and destructive personal vices. I will honor the gift of life by keeping myself sexually pure and free from addictive drugs.

I will seek to be godly in all things, Christlike in all relationships

"Therefore, as God's chosen people, holy and dearly loved, clothe yourselves with compassion, kindness, humility, gentleness and patience. Bear with each other and forgive whatever grievances you may have against one another. Forgive as the Lord forgave you. And over all these virtues put on love, which binds them all together in perfect unity." Colossians 3:12-14

In every relationship and in every situation, I will seek to live as Christ would. I will work to heal brokenness, to value each person as a child of God, to avoid petty quarrels and harsh words, to let go of bitterness and resentment that hinder genuine Christian love.

Foreword
by Louie Giglio, Founder Passion Ministries

God labored six days to create the heavens and the earth. If only the making of a godly man were that easy. But it's not. The galaxies God could do in a phrase, yet the journey toward Christlikeness is man's lifelong pursuit. It just goes to show how deeply the stain of sin runs through the human soul.

Created by and for God, we are so willfully bent away from Him. Convinced that we can live above His laws and outside His love, we rely on our own strength and wisdom to lead us home. The results are always disastrous, short-changing the soul made only for Him and leaving wounded lives in our wake. Even worse, our fallen minds suffer from major short term memory disorder, leading us to repeat our mistakes in spite of the pain and disappointment they bring.

But, thank God we are not irrevocably mired in the limitations of sinful humanity. In fact, God has more for us than our minds can imagine. The apostle Paul, the transformed man himself, tells us that God's desire is to conform us into the very image of Jesus. (Rom. 8:29). Now that's a "God-statement" if there ever was one. From the twisted wreckage of the human heart God intends to forge a new man, one made in the likeness of His Son.

But how? Through nothing short of the radical life, death and resurrection of Christ. He died to free us, yet came out of the tomb not just to show His power, but to give us hope. For Paul continues, ". . . that He (Jesus) might be the firstborn of many brothers." (Rom. 9:29b). Do you see it? We, too, can walk in the power of His resurrection life!

Make no mistake, godly character is not easy. But it is possible.

What Gregg does so well in this book is to take the reader down a determined and disciplined path, one that allows him to understand and experience the realities of Christ's death and His life each step of the way. Who better to write such a book than one who lives with the goal of godly character so clearly in his sites, pouring faithfully from what he's learned into the lives of thousands of young followers of Jesus every week. Written from Gregg's "real-life" perspective, these insights are both practical and profitable for the man who desires to successfully navigate the college scene. Let him lead you. You'll be glad you did.

Registration Line Begins Here!

As we begin this journey for the highest education, becoming a godly man feels a little like the first day of class. The pages of this book are crisp and clean, no highlights or blanks filled in, just a fresh start with much knowledge to gain. On that first day the prof usually hands out the syllabus to give the vision for the days to come. The sheet shows what must be learned in order to finish the class victoriously. Thankfully, the grade at the end of this course won't be something for your GPA, but for your heart. The goal is for you to become a godly man. Webster's dictionary beautifully defines the word:

godly-adj. filled with love for God.

That's the A+ for us, to be filled with love for God in every aspect of college life. So, here's our syllabus for the days and pages to come: a godly man is one who loves God with his friendships, romances, battles with temptation, finances, direction in his life and time. This book offers something textbooks can't, a deeper and more intimate relationship with the Highest Educator Himself.

In order to get all that you can out of this study, I want to encourage you to do the following:
- Begin each session praying for the Holy Spirit to speak clearly to you.
- Thoughtfully answer the questions asked and fill in the blanks as directed.
- Give proper respect to the Bible. Look up the passages you're directed to and read closely the ones already printed out for you.
- Lastly, personalize this book by writing your thoughts or insights you've gained in the margins. Get to know Jesus Christ deeply as you journey and journal.

Grab a pen and your Bible, take a seat on the couch, at the kitchen table, or with a bunch of friends and get ready to meet with Him for a semester lifetime of the highest education of becoming a godly man.

Friendships: The Four Amigos

Friendships: The Four Amigos

Think back to your first day in a college classroom for just a moment. Do you remember the emotional spectrum you were feeling that day as a college freshman? Fear and excitement, nervousness and wonder were probably typical reactions if you were like me. Texas A&M is a huge place, and I seemed so insignificant in those initial days.

After cramming 4 years into 4 1/2, my feet entered my last class at Texas A&M. Thinking about the one major difference between the beginning and the end was more than the rewards of a college education. It was the treasure chest of friendships over those years.

Do you remember your first day in the college classroom? What were your emotions that day? Jot down one or two.

1.
2.

With college in the rearview mirror and working in a ministry for college students, I've come to realize one thing about students: they are "wired up" for relationships. God has placed in all of us a desire for relationships, and college offers numerous places to meet that desire, like . . .

[ ] Dorm Life
[ ] Dating Relationships
[ ] Classes
[ ] Social Events
[ ] Work
[ ] Athletics/Intramurals
[ ] Church
[ ] Fraternities
[ ] Organizations
[ ] Other _____

> College students are "wired up" for relationships.

Check all the boxes above where you have formed previous or current relationships.

Through a wide variety of social interaction, college becomes an agenda overflowing with class projects, Bible studies, organizational meetings, intramural tournaments and social events. One by one, each of these allows a constant flow of friendships (some short-lived, others long-lasting) throughout our college career. Those relationships leave behind one of two results: 1) They build us up and make us more like Christ or 2) They tear us down and make us less like Him.

Sandpaper on the Heart

Located in all home improvement stores is an item common to the carpenter or cabinet-builder . . . sandpaper. In numerous shapes and sizes, the value of the sandpaper lies in its grit. Sheets of heavier grit will conquer layers of old varnish while extra fine grit is used for the final touch. No matter the intensity, the outcome is the same . . . change!

Do you believe other people have an influence on our lives? [ ] Yes   [ ] No

How about in our walk with Christ? [ ] Yes   [ ] No

Share an example of how you have seen this to be true.

Our relationships are no different. In a trade of interaction we take turns placing the grit of our life up against another's, sanding positively or negatively, but always resulting in someone changed. Some friends sand completely with the grain, bringing out the natural beauty that is below the surface. God uses them to round the edges and smooth the corners of our lives. The result? We look more like Christ because of them. Other friends sand against the grain, roughing us up and shaping us in a negative way.

Do any of these situations sound familiar:
- When I hang out with _____ I always seem to start cussing or tell a dirty joke.
- When I hang out with _____ we always end up at a party.
- When I hang out with _____ I have a hard time being me.

The luster and shine begin to vanish from the surface.

Paul's Amigos

Read 2 Timothy 4:9-15.
List the eight people Paul mentions:

1. _____
2. _____
3. _____
4. _____
5. _____
6. _____
7. _____
8. _____

This is one of those passages in the Bible that seems unimportant and often gets overlooked. Don't you wish sometimes they had more familiar names so we could understand, much less pronounce them? You know, like, "Bob from Texas gave a letter to Donna for delivery to the church in Kansas." Too easy though! So, we must dig deeper and pay close attention. The names are different and the locations are unusual, but the truth is incredible.

In this role call of biblical players, four separate groups of men are mentioned that have a distinct relationship with Paul. All made a definite impact on him, but in different ways. The interesting point is that these four groups are as real today on our college campus as they were for Paul in 67 AD.

Paul's Four Amigos

Intersecting: Friends during a certain season of life—not mergers but intersections (Crescens, Titus, and Tychicus)

Faithful: Close lifelong friends; people who are a part of life for an extended period of time, many seasons; they merge with you as you go through life (Luke)

Backslidden: They used to walk with Christ but they have gotten off the path. (Demas)

Opposing: Their actions and words are opposed to Christianity and as a result, it strains the relationship you have with them because you are a representative of Christ. (Alexander)

Amigo #1

Intersecting Friends: Friends during a certain season of life—not mergers but intersections

The first group of friends in Paul's life are intersecting friends—Crescens, Titus and Tychicus (v.10). These guys were rock solid in desiring to build the kingdom.

For the record . . .
- Crescens was one of the 72 people that Jesus sent out in Luke 10.
- Titus was the guy who delivered the letter of 2 Corinthians and served the church there.
- Tychicus delivered the letters of Ephesians and Colossians that are in your Bible today.

These men were intersections in Paul's life. They came through for a missionary journey, grabbed a letter and took off. Entering for just a short time in Paul's life, they sanded each other into the image of Christ, taking the opportunity to round the corners and smooth the edges with godly companionship.

How do your intersecting friends impact you today?

There are people that God will place at intersections in our lives. They're not mergers staying for an extended period. They're intersections. They're friendships that enter at a certain stage of our lives, and then they're gone. The result of that relationship can bring different results:

- Positive (Build Up): Their time in our life blesses and encourages us or we bless and encourage them.
- Negative (Tear Down): We make some of our worst decisions while they are in our lives.

Result #1: They build us up.

God often places someone at a camp, a club, or a church as a certain intersection to build you up. Someone to say something that you'll never forget or to encourage you at a moment of need. I've seen that in my life.

How many times have these positive intersections taken place in your college career?

- You get in class and have someone sit next to you, and you are best buds by the end of the semester. You're tight. You're exchanging notes when you miss days of class. You're hanging out together cramming for finals, and then the end of the semester comes, your classes change and you rarely see him again. Then when you do see him, the extent of the relationship dwindles to a "Hello."
- Or maybe you sign up for a small group Bible study or attend a men's conference with guys from your church. You invest several days or several weeks in prayer or study with them. Then the study ends or the weekend is over and the relationships you made peaked out in those few days. You remember them and might even continue praying for them. But as far as the relationship going beyond an intersection in your life . . . it just doesn't happen.

Give an example and description of a positive "intersection" in your life:

Take just a moment and write out this verse in your own words.

1 Thessalonians 5:11

Result #2: They tear us down.

Unfortunately, some of the worst decisions of our lives are made at intersections. Years later, we wonder how that person ever convinced us that this was actually "fun," "a good time" or "what everyone else was doing." The result is not godly companionship but a skeleton in the closet.

Common remarks of the destructive intersection:
- "Come on man, everybody's doing it."
- "It'll be alright; just have one."
- "Let's go back to your place."

Have you ever wondered where that person is today? That dating relationship that went too far or that friendship that led you astray. Most likely these were just intersections in high school or college. But before we realize it, we are less like Christ than when we began because of this intersection.

Give an example and description of a negative "intersection" in your life:

Have you dealt with God about this issue? [ ] Yes   [ ] No

Write out the following verses in a paraphrased format:
> Proverbs 27:6

> Proverbs 19:4

Amigo #2

Faithful Friends: Close lifelong friends; people who are a part of life for an extended period of time, many seasons; they merge with you as you go through life

The second amigo found in verse 11 is a faithful friend. Take note: there are three intersecting friends and only one faithful friend. There will be literally hundreds of intersecting friends in your life, but there will be very few faithful friends. Some intersecting friends will become faithful friends, but most will not. Faithful friends are few and far between. They're a rare commodity. College is the place where most of our closest friendships develop. Usually through roommates (if a faithful enemies situation doesn't arise), fraternity brothers, or teammates, we form a bond that blesses us for life.

13

Examples from my life

Troy and I met in our sixth grade homeroom. Each day we talked about things of eternal significance—Jenny Laster and video games. Being such great friends, we both asked Jenny to "go with us" at the same time. Literally, we looked at each other, counted to three, and in unison asked, "Will you go with me?" She said yes to him and "You're too good of a friend" to me, code for "Not in a million years." He and Jenny broke up a couple days later because he was to scared to call her, but Troy and I remained friends. At the end of the year we even won the "Three Stooges Award" from our teachers. The third stooge was just an intersection. I haven't talk to him in years.

Brett and I first met in fifth grade but didn't talk much until a high school art class. At that point we decided to share a room in college. The conversations as we fell asleep covered every subject from the cute girl across the street, who we referred to as "Lady X" because we didn't know her name, to who should win the Heisman. Our relationship grew and grew, and over time became a faithful friendship.

List a faithful friend or two:
   1.
   2.

Read 2 Timothy 4:11-12.
Who is Paul's faithful friend that remained by his side? Check your answer.
   [ ] Tychicus   [ ] Mark   [ ] Luke

The apostle Paul in all his power and prestige, a leader in the Jewish synagogue and now the Christian church says, "Only Luke is with me." That's it. One faithful friend is all he mentions. Despite Paul's past and all his baggage, despite the missionary life and the growing critics that wanted him dead, Luke hung tough and remained true to his friend. He was grit that left a shine . . . a faithful friend. Friendships like that don't come around every day, and they rarely come in abundance.

List two reasons why faithful friends are difficult to find.
   1.
   2.

Why is it important to have faithful friends?

List three attributes below of someone you consider a faithful friend:
   1.
   2.
   3.

Read Proverbs 18:24.

Amigo #3

Backsliding friends: They used to walk with Christ but they have strayed off the path.

Fill in the blank for 2 Timothy 4:10.
"For _____, because he loved this world, has deserted me and gone to Thessalonica."

If there is a verse of Scripture I could speak on once a week for the rest of my life, this is it. I think about Demas all the time. This isn't the only reference where he can be found.

Philemon 23, 24
"Epaphras, my fellow prisoner in Christ Jesus, sends you greetings. And so do Mark, Aristarchus, Demas and Luke, my fellow workers."

Demas was one of Paul's right hand men, a fixture in the inner circle, a "big dog" in the kingdom. Then what? Doesn't it break your heart? It does mine. Paul writes, "But Demas, having loved this world, has deserted me and gone to Thessalonica." The man once committed to the call and faithful is now out of the game and searching.

Demas is a backsliding friend. Someone who used to be walking, and now is stumbling. Someone who used to be running the race with Christ but now is riding the pine. The reason I could speak about Demas, day in and day out, is because I want with everything I have, not to be a Demas.

What causes a backsliding lifestyle? Here are a couple of hints:
- The name "Demas" in the Greek means "popular."
- Thessalonica at that time was the party town of Northern Israel.

What do I do about my backsliding friends?

Sadly, some of our friends are going to bail on their walk with God. They will slowly get too busy for God or allow sin to dominate their life, and before you know it God is nowhere to be found in their life. What do we do in those instances? Our role is not to remain idle, but to pray and obey. Pray for them, lift them up to God, that He would break their hearts and bring them home. Obey, as the Lord asks you to reach out. Invite them to church, call them and see what's going on in their lives; see if they want to grab a movie. Be a friend—not a preacher. Ask them how their walk with Christ is, and then don't lecture. Just listen. Just like the prodigal son in Luke 16, you never know when they might be ready to come back to the Father.

List a couple of backsliding friends in your life:

1.
2.

Write out a prayer for them in the space below:

How can you make contact with them this week? Jot down at least three ideas. Could you invite them to church or lunch, call them up, email them, etc?

1.
2.
3.

Amigo #4

Opposing Friends: Their actions and words are opposed to Christianity, and as a result it strains your relationship because thankfully, they see you as a representative of Christ.

Timothy 4:14 describes our last amigo, Alexander, an opposing friend. There are five Alexanders mentioned in the New Testament. Let's take a brief look at them.

1. The father of Simon who carried the cross of Christ. (Mark 15:21)
2. A relative of Annas the high priest of the Sanhedrin. He was present as Peter and John were questioned about how they healed the crippled beggar. 30 AD (Acts 4:6)
3. A Jew thrust forth as the spokesmen during the riot in Ephesus over Paul's preaching concerning the goddess Artemis. 58 AD (Acts 19:33)
4. The one Paul handed over to Satan along with Hymenaeus. (1 Tim. 1:20)
5. The metalworker who did Paul a great deal of harm. (2 Tim. 4:14)

Alexander represents the people in your life who will be completely opposed to the gospel. By word and action, their beliefs are in direct opposition with our own.

Are these examples from your collegiate experience?

- Professors who think Christianity is on the same level as Santa Claus or mythology.
- Opposing friends who think you're crazy to wait until marriage.
- Friends who think you are out of your mind to go across the ocean to reach the world or across town to the homeless shelter to serve food to the hungry.
- People who, in whatever shape or form, discard any part of the Bible as their guide.

There are two ways God uses opposing friends.

1) We gain depth in our faith. These people stretch us and challenge our own beliefs, forcing us to know what we believe and why. They sand us with heavier grit in their opposition, but the result for us is always depth.

2) They are great ministry opportunities. Believe it or not, our relationships with opposing friends are some of the best places of ministry. Most of those who are truly against God have reasons for their (dis)belief and enjoy dialoguing about the subject. It often makes for interesting and challenging conversation.

List some opposing friends in your life.
1.
2.
3.

How can you witness or minister to them this week?

Write out a prayer for them in the space below.

Which Group is Yours?

Now that we've uncovered the four amigos (intersecting, faithful, backsliding and opposing), let me ask you this: Which group would your friends put you in? Would they say, "Oh, John? He's a Demas." "Chris . . . opposing." Maybe they would say faithful or intersecting.

Now, in which group do most of your friends fit?

Circle the group (or groups) you typically gravitate to.
   Intersecting   Faithful   Opposing   Backsliding

In the Middle of the Tension

Let me tell you where God wants us. He wants us smack dab in the middle of the tension, having friends from each group. Being sandpaper and also being sanded. Receiving, but also giving. The tension is uncomfortable and it won't always be easy or make sense, but it provides fertile ground for God's life changing work.

In the spring semester of my freshman year I was living in the tension. Brett and I shared an apartment with two other guys, Jimmy and Gary. We all got along fine but our walks with Christ weren't on the same page. Brett and I were growing more than we ever had. Memory verses on the wall, Bibles on the nightstand, and even a corkboard full of pictures of backsliding or opposing friends we were praying for. Jimmy was a great guy but thought we had taken this Jesus stuff a little too far, while Gary was flat out opposed. All factions seemed to be represented. At times Gary would argue, challenging Brett and me on every issue from evolution to sex. We would answer and point him to a verse. The Holy Spirit began to work. By the end of the year the walls were coming down. The opposition slowly gave way to curiosity and Gary became a Christian. Today he pastors a church, has three kids and a godly wife. The tension of opposition was tough that semester, but God used Brett and me to sand the calluses off of Gary's heart. The end result: a life was changed then, and more are changed each Sunday morning!

SPIRITUAL GROWTH

Three Ingredients that will Impact our Four Amigos

Read 2 Timothy 4:16,17.

Did you identify the three ingredients of friendship addressed by Paul that pertain to friends, family, or dating relationships? Those ingredients are:
1. Forgiveness
2. Foundation
3. Focus

Forgiveness

The first ingredient we must examine in relationships is a heart of forgiveness. Paul says in verse 16 that in his first defense no one stood at his side, but may it not be held against them. That first defense he's talking about is recorded in Acts 22, when he stood before the Caesar of Rome, on trial for being a Christian. Paul presented and proved his faith during his trial, but no other Christians chose to support his claims. They remained seated with lips sealed, while he stood alone in defense of his faith. His reaction could have been bitterness and resentment, but he chose to forgive.

WITNESS

From a petty charge to a felony offense, our reaction must be similar to Paul's. Why? That is the attitude Jesus Christ commanded us to have. Throughout Scripture it is evident that forgiveness is not an option with Jesus. For example:
- When asked how many times a person should forgive, Jesus responds, "seventy times seven" (Matt. 18:21).
- "If your brother sins, rebuke him, and if he repents, forgive him. If he sins against you seven times in a day, and seven times comes back to you and says, 'I repent,' forgive him" (Luke 17:3).

Easier said than done, right! Especially when we are left hanging by our friends like Paul or dumped on by roommate or family. A heart of forgiveness becomes a test of our own faith. We must take on a Christlike attitude that says, "Even though you blew it, I forgive you." It's crucial to a healthy relationship. So often we hold grudges that escalate from aggravation to anger to bitterness, only because we wanted to be right more than make the situation right. The end result is pride in our own heart. What could have been dissolved in forgiveness is now a wedge between you and _____.

Is there a name that crosses your mind when you see that blank?

Below are a few situations that call for our forgiveness. Do any sound familiar to you?
- Your roommate never takes out the trash or does the dishes.
- Your parents get a divorce after decades of marriage.
- A friend asks the girl out who he knows you like.
- A brother or sister gets all the help and you get none.

Is there a friend you need to forgive? If so for what?
Who _____   For what _____

Is there a friend you need to ask forgiveness from? If so for what?
Who _____   For what _____

Forgiveness: At the root of a relationship with Jesus

It's amazing to think what our world would be like if we all made forgiveness a habit. What's even more amazing than that is the model of forgiveness we have in Jesus Christ. When Jesus died on the cross, He died with "forgiveness" in mind. At the end of that thought was you and me! The root of our relationship with Jesus is built on a foundation of forgiving blood. He paid the ultimate price so you and I might inherit eternity. When we forgive, we are a living example of the love Christ showed us on Calvary.

Foundation

"But the Lord stood at my side and gave me strength" (2 Tim. 4:17).

What's the foundation of your friendships? Is it a common interest, organization, degree plan, or is it Jesus Christ?

Our key relationship can't be a strong Christian friend, although that would be great. It can't be a girlfriend or fiancée who loves Jesus, although that would be a blessing. It can't even be a Christian organization or a close group of accountability partners, though all of these are wonderful. Only one relationship can be at the center of who we are and what we're becoming: our relationship with Jesus Christ!

19

Look at the following activity. Match each topic and statement on the left with the Scripture that relates to it on the right.

___ LUST – Fall deeply in love with Him and He'll be your companion.   a. (1 John 2:15-17)

___ CONTENTMENT – Trust Him for provision and He'll be your resource.   b. (Ps. 33:1-3)

___ MUSIC – Turn off the world and He'll give you a new song.   c. (Col. 3:3-5)

___ ALCOHOL – Get drunk on the Spirit and He'll fill you with joy.   d. (Eph. 5:18)

___ PORNOGRAPHY – Fix your eyes on Christ and He'll show you eternity.   e. (Ps. 37:23-24)

___ FOUL LANGUAGE – Praise Him with your mouth and He'll bring healing.   f. (2 Cor. 4:18)

___ SETBACKS – Hope in Jesus and He'll give you perseverance.   g. (Rom. 5: 3-5)

___ YOUR PAST – Hide in Christ and He'll forget your past.   h. (Pr. 12-18)

a: LUST e: CONTENTMENT b: MUSIC d: ALCOHOL f: PORNOGRAPHY h: FOUL LANGUAGE g: SETBACKS c: YOUR PAST

No guy or girl, friend or family member can provide the ultimate strength we need for life. God may use them to speak to you. He may use a faithful friend for wise counsel. He may bring an intersection to spur you on in your faith. But there's only one who walks by our side and gives us strength beyond human limitations . . . Jesus!

Focus

Fill in the blank from 2 Timothy 4:17. "But the Lord stood by my side and gave me strength, so that _____.

Without question, fun and enjoyment are great aspects of friendship, but they are not the focus. The focus is the message of Christ. Now does this mean preach 24/7, never talk about anything but God, and live at church? No, it means sharing Christ in our words and actions to the backslidden and opposed; sanding and being sanded to the intersecting and faithful. It's finding your niche in the tension and being salt and light with your life. This means we must continue to grow in Christ for the message of His life to be fully proclaimed through us. That message of forgiveness, love and grace is what our "four amigos" need from us.

CHRISTLIKE
RELATIONSHIPS

Read 1 Corinthians 3:6 and fill in the blank:
"I (Paul) planted the seed, Apollos watered it, but _____ made it grow."
Rank the focus of most of your friendships.
     ___ Fun
     ___ Growth in Christ
     ___ Major in school
     ___ Sports
     ___ Similar interests (i.e. organizations, athletics, or how free time is spent)
Is it difficult for you to have an eternal focus in friendships? If so, why?

Don't ever give up

I have a friend I used to party with in high school. Numerous times, I've shared the message of Christ with him, all resulting in a "no thanks" response. I'm now entering year 13 of sharing, praying and loving my friend. It has been a long road with no fruit, but just recently I asked, "What are your thoughts about Christ in this problem?" He responded by saying he had been giving it some thought and knows he needs something more out of life. Thirteen years of presenting the message and letting God handle the response, and we still aren't all the way there. But I'll never give up!

Three ingredients for four amigos:
- **Forgiveness** – "At my first defense, no one came to my support . . . May it not be held against them" (2 Tim. 4:16).
- **Foundation** – "But the Lord stood at my side and gave me strength," (2 Tim. 4:17a,b).
- **Focus** – "so that through me the message might be fully proclaimed and all the Gentiles might hear it" (2 Tim. 4:17c).

When we live a life that is built on the forgiveness, foundation, and focus of Christ, we leave an eternal impact on our four amigo groups.

Encourage Your Group

1. Why is it often more of a challenge for men to develop close friendships than women?

2. Which amigo group is the biggest joy or trial in your life? Why?

3. Fill in the blanks: I would be a better friend if I quit _____ and started _____.

4. List some ways this group can grow closer as friends, i.e. go to a game, eat out, play ultimate frisbee one afternoon, email, etc.

5. Pick one of the suggestions from the previous question and do it this week.
   Activity _____ Date _____ Time _____

Between You and God

1. Ask God if you are usually "sanded" in a positive or negative way by your friends. What answer did you receive from Him?

2. Tell God you are seeking to know how friendships can encourage growth in your walk with Him.

Dating: Wanting, Wishing, and Waiting

Dating: Wanting, Wishing, and Waiting

As I reflect back on my college days, one area consumed much of my heart and mind . . . **dating**. In fact, before I met Kelly I spent many hours thinking (like most guys) about who I should date, what qualities would be compatible with mine and wondering when God was going to deliver "The One." Like no other area of a college man's life, the opposite sex is the primary focus during these years. Do you remember how it all started? Possibly junior high, when she—the same girl you've known since elementary school—all of a sudden was pretty. The notes exchanged hands, and you both checked YES on the question: Will you go with me? It usually lasted long enough to attend one school dance together, then it was over. She left you in the dust for your best friend. Oh, well. Those were the days.

In what grade did you first discover that girls were okay?

What style did you use to ask out your first girlfriend? (Check the one that applies.)

[ ] You asked her to check YES or NO.
[ ] You had a friend call her for you.
[ ] You actually had guts and asked her face to face.
[ ] What do you mean? I'm still looking!
[ ] You _____
                    (Fill in your story.)

In case you didn't know, that isn't the way to capture a college girl's heart. The stakes are higher now, the asking-out more complex and the risk heightened. All of a sudden those seven digits on the phone to her apartment make our palms sweaty and heart race. The fact still remains: girls are the object of a godly man's desire. We will do just about anything to get the girl of our dreams. In fact, some efforts can even be categorized as abnormal. Like . . .

- Wearing cologne
- Opening the car door
- Talking on the phone for hours
- Writing letters
- Wearing khakis instead of jeans
- Walking the mall

The list above is an impressive list and a quick way to a woman's heart, but it lacks the most important dating credential: putting God first in your dating life. Whether you are wanting, wishing, or waiting for a relationship, or you're on the verge of marriage, it's never too soon or too late to hear what God has to say about the issue of dating.

Dating: Wanting, Wishing, and Waiting

SESSION 2

Wanting

The deep desire for the companionship that resonates throughout our heart, soul, thoughts, plans and lifestyle. This "want" can effect us in both positive and negative ways.

Examine your source of companionship through the years:
- Infancy and early childhood – parents, siblings
- Elementary school – parents, siblings, teachers, and classmates
- Junior high and high school – friends (teammates, youth group, peer group), family, teachers
- College – mentors, professors, faithful friends (But a new category is on the horizon: a wife, or at least a serious girlfriend)

"Wanting" the next chapter in life is a natural part of being a college student. We enter as teenagers desiring fun and friends and exit as adults tired of the game. We spend four to five years in college wrapped up in this search, and walk across the stage ready for the real world, a real job, a real paycheck, and for many of us, a real companion. The challenge is keeping that desire in the proper perspective.

The Misdiagnosed "Want"

Proper diagnosis: The desire for a companion is a natural part of who you are. It is not wrong or sinful when kept in the proper perspective.
Misdiagnosis: When our desire for a companion is greater than our desire for Jesus, then our perspective is wrong and the result can be sinful.

The woman at the well misdiagnosed her greatest need. Read John 4:7-18.

What was she replacing the companionship of God with?

> "The hunger for love is much harder to remove than the hunger for bread."
> —Mother Teresa

The scene at the well portrays a woman who's really not unlike you and me. At some point in her life it stands to reason that she had a "want" for a relationship. Why? Maybe she longed for security, love, belonging, or someone to fill the lonely hours of singleness. Whatever the reason, the void was misdiagnosed and her "want" was filled with five marriages and an affair. The result for the woman was a thirst that could not be quenched by companionship alone. Her options were the same as ours today: Drink of the desire for companionship and be thirsty, or drink of Jesus, the living Water, and never thirst.

In what ways have you misdiagnosed the "wants" in your soul?

If a new parable were to be written called "The man at the well," and you were that man, what area of your life would Jesus point to as a misdiagnosed want?

Have you ever looked to dating to fill the "want" of your heart?
    [ ] Yes   [ ] No   [ ] Not Sure

Misdirected actions

The woman at the well had a thirst that could only be met by Christ alone. Her failure to surrender that area of her life led her misdiagnosed "want" into misdirected actions. When we choose the contentment and love of a girlfriend to fill the longing of our heart over Jesus, we are setting our feet on a dangerous path. The result is a direction of actions that provide less than God's best in dating.

Dating misdirected actions:

1) Your dating standards will be lowered.
If you are subconsciously looking for someone to fill the void of dating, girls will become a life raft you cling to. Instead of wanting God's best for us, we take the next girl to come along to feed our desire for a relationship.

Describe a time you or a friend lowered the dating standards to fill the void.

How did this affect your/their focus on Christ?

2) You'll seek the external instead of the eternal.
1) Unrealistic expectations on the girl
Only seeing the external of a girl and not the eternal is like driving full speed down a dead end street. Proverbs 11:22 says, "Like a gold ring in a pig's snout is a beautiful woman who shows no discretion." The external isn't the focus and good looks aren't the acid test. The visual is important to us, but the unseen is what is important to God. Rest assured the heart of a woman is more important than the figure. Proverbs 31:30 says, "Charm is deceptive, and beauty is fleeting; but a woman who fears the Lord is to be praised." Often guys will date a physical "10" and a spiritual "2" without a second thought. Believe me, I'm all for 10s! My wife is the most beautiful woman in the world, but her heart is what I'm most interested in.

What is your idea of a spiritual "10" in a girl?

2) Unrealistic expectations on the guy

Pressure on the external isn't reserved for females; we also place it on ourselves. At 5' 8", and a buck-fifty, I'm not exactly chiseled. To remedy this, I've joined the same gym three times, only to waste my effort in a short-lived pursuit of the "perfect" physique. Have you been there? Maybe it was in other ways, like desiring the right clothes, the right car, or the right pair of shades. Or possibly trying to be "Joe Cool" around the girls. Putting up a front of actions or words, when the real you is locked inside and screaming to come out. The bottom line is . . . our exterior will not get us more mileage than our interior.

- "For physical training is of some value, but godliness has value for all things, holding promise for both the present life and the life to come" (1 Tim. 4:8).

- "Therefore we do not lose heart. Though outwardly we are wasting away, yet inwardly we are being renewed day by day. So we fix our eyes not on what is seen, but on what is unseen. For what is seen is temporary, but what is unseen is eternal" (2 Cor. 4:16,18).

How do you incorrectly emphasize external beauty in girls, and how can this create misdirection in your dating life?

How do you incorrectly emphasize the external in yourself?

3) You'll place too much pressure on the relationship.

When Christ fails to be the center of your life, pressure has a tendency to escalate in a relationship both physically and emotionally. Boundaries are crossed when spiritual maturity is lacked and the sole focus becomes the feeling you get when together. The physical aspects (like holding hands, kissing, saying "I love you" too soon) take center stage, until it is 70mph in a 35mph zone and life is out of control. The innocence numbs both parties' ability to think clearly, as the desire to please each other outweighs pleasing God.

One bit of advice: Slow down! Only one thing needs to be decided on date number one: will there be a date number two? Relationships take time to grow. The reality of God's plan will not be revealed in a relationship that doesn't honor Him. The best investment you can make in a girl is 1) putting Christ first in your life and 2) allowing enough time for the real you and the real her to be revealed.

> "The deepest principle in the human nature is the craving to be appreciated."
> —William James

the highest education:
becoming a godly man

When relationships move too fast . . . (Check all that apply)

[ ] Poor decisions are made.
[ ] The physical aspects get really difficult to control.
[ ] The carefree fun begins to become work.
[ ] We grow numb to God's plan for the relationship.
[ ] All is well . . . buy the diamond.

Have you experienced other ways that dating can become misdirected? Explain.

Properly Diagnosing the Want

Check out John 4:13 and paraphrase it below:

Jesus Christ gives us the ultimate thirst-quencher in this verse: **living water**. He doesn't claim bottled water can do it, a protein smoothie, nor any drink of your choice. It's only a drink from the fountain of God Himself. The Samaritan woman had been lining up at the well of humanity all her life, only to come up dry and thirsty. Don't fall into that trap! The Greek translation for Holy Spirit is the word *Paraclete,* which means "One who walks alongside of." Properly diagnosing our "wants" will begin when we allow the Paraclete to do His job, to walk beside us in our single life, to guide us to the right companion, to be our measuring stick of obedience in dating and most importantly to lead us to choose the right well—the one of **living water.**

How can discovering the "Paraclete" fill your "want" for a girlfriend?

Who's the love of your life?

On campus one day I pulled up to a stop sign and looked at the people in the car next to me. It was a girl and a guy going on a date. First, I felt jealous, thinking, "Why not me Lord? I'm a good guy trying to seek You daily. That guy probably isn't even a Christian; it's just not fair." It's amazing the thoughts that can go through my mind just at a stop sign. I would have needed three years of counseling if it had been a stop light! But finally my heart clicked into the right frame of reference and I began to pray. "Lord, I want to long for You like I do for a girlfriend. In Your timing provide her, but as for now You, Jesus, are my want and desire. May I fall more in love with You today." Then I drove off singing a praise song that became my theme for singleness.

> *You're the love of my life*
> *You're the joy of my morning.*
> *You're the song in my heart,*
> *And I will praise your Holy name.*
> *Copyright 1990 Mark Gungor*

Isaiah puts it like this: "Come, all you who are thirsty, come to the waters; and you who have no money, come, buy and eat! Come, buy wine and milk without money and without cost. Why spend money on what is not bread, and your labor on what does not satisfy? Listen, listen to me, and eat what is good, and your soul will delight in the richest of fare" (Isa. 55:1-2).

Christ was the love of my life then and still is today, though dating has now resulted in marriage. The song just mentioned was sung during my wedding to declare to all those in attendance that day: "Even though God has provided an incredible wife for me, He is still my first love." He is my living Water and the Well I choose. He is the Paraclete who walks beside me in life. He is the answer to the "wants" of my life.

Why is it important to properly diagnose the want?

Wishing

Wishing is a natural part of growing up. Think back to your youth and the flurry of wishes that at some point went through your mind. Like . . .
- Please Lord, it's the bottom of the 9th and I need a hit.
- Man when I grow up, I am going to be a _____.

(Fill in your answer)

And now our wish list has taken on a real-world flair designed for adults. Like . . .
- Lord, help me complete these last 15 hours of class so I can get a real job.
- For once, give me a roommate who can wash his own dishes and clean his room.
- I wish I had someone cute, fun, and godly to hang out with.

Our wish list is constantly changing with each stage of life we are in, from the baseball games that are now intramurals for most of us, to the freedom that first car brought to our lives. Each of us has a history of wishes that now decorate our past. But the one wish that "tops the list" of our future is the wish for "The One" to enter our life. Thoughts like, "Will she go out with me?" "How will I know if she's the one?" and, "My parents didn't succeed in marriage, will I?" matter more than winning a little league game. In this section we are going to identify and define the wishes of a godly man for a godly woman.

Let's get real. Write down your wish list and be honest. What are you looking for in a girl?

1.	6.
2.	7.
3.	8.
4.	9.
5.	10.

Now go back through and put an * next to the non-negotiables, the things that have to be there. Put a + by the ones that would be nice.

Genesis 24: The following is a wish list Abraham had for finding his son Isaac a wife:

- In the family (Gen. 24:1-9)
- Servant's heart (not "me first" mentality) (Gen. 24:12-14)
- Trusted God (Left home to be obedient) (Gen. 24:58)
- Respectful: Respected her husband (Gen. 24:64,65)

In the Family

Read Genesis 24:1-9.

Abraham places the first parameter on the wish list: If she is not in the family then she's not the one for my son. This criteria is expressed in the New Testament in 2 Corinthians 6:14, "Do not be yoked together with unbelievers." Basically, the first item on the wish list for a Christian guy is that she is a Christian girl. She's a part of the family of God. Is this to say only Christian girls are cute, nice, or sweet? Not at all! But for someone to earn your companionship, they're going to have to believe in the same God.

A girl under the leadership of Christ, a daughter of His, has a resource for love that can't be rivaled by her worldly counterpart. Her salvation in Christ means she has humbled herself before God allowing His blood to wash her clean. "The old has gone, the new has come" (2 Cor. 5:17).

What should the primary priority of the wish list be? Why?

A Servant's Heart

Read Genesis 24:12-21.

The chief servant's prayer in verses 12-14 in regard to a prospective wife weren't for great looks, a family fortune, or a nice wardrobe. He desired one thing for Isaac: a servant. A woman who would put God first, others second, and herself last. Rebekah passed the test. She didn't know the implications of the day. She didn't know this trip to the well would be any different than the days and years before. Without any reservation she served the stranger, choosing service over selfishness and as a result, answered his prayer.

Guys, don't miss this. If you want to be loved for who you are; if you want to know what it means to have a godly wife; if you desire to be encouraged in your walk, supported in your job, comforted in your failures, and become all God desires you to be in life, **find a godly woman of service.** A woman who has been forgiven and set free. A woman who says, "You first" not "Me first." A woman who doesn't just attend church, but loves the church and the body of Christ. A woman whose hands can hold a baby and dig a ditch. A woman who lives by Scripture, is fueled by prayer, and is enthralled in worship. A woman like Rebekah, who walks daily with the Lord and loves His people.

Other great women of service:

Ruth –
A "woman of noble character" (Ruth 3:11).

Tryphena and Tryphosa –
"Those women who work hard in the Lord" (Rom. 16:12).

Rahab –
Was spared death "because she hid the men Joshua had sent . . . to Jericho" (Josh. 6:25).

Esther -
A woman of great beauty and intelligence, she saved the Jews from annihilation by Haman the Agagite. (The book of Esther)

Deborah –
Was a prophetess, mother, and leader of Israel all at once (Judges 4—5)

Mary (Mother of Jesus) –
Called "highly favored," and "the Lord's servant," gave birth to the Son of God, Jesus Christ. (The Gospels)

Trusted God

Read Genesis 24:54-61.
Rebekah is batting 1.000 so far, but here comes the curve ball . . . "Will you go with this man?" **"I will go,"** she replied. "Sorry mom, brother, homeland, comfort zone . . . I'm going for it." The day had come. A girl had become a woman and a world was waiting. A camel ride and a foreign land; escorted by a bunch of men; a husband in waiting whom she had never met or seen. What was this woman thinking? One word—**trust!**

It wasn't logical and didn't make much sense. God's timing was a test of Rebekah's trust, and she responded with a home run response: "I will go."

A Christian girl and a godly woman are miles apart. Many girls and guys claim faith in God, but when the going gets tough or God calls them to a task, they hit the road. The comfort zone feels too nice. The risk seems too great. Responding "I will go" to God's plan for our lives takes more than weekly church attendance; it takes real trusting of God. Trusting as in Proverbs 3:5, "Trust in the Lord with all your heart and lean not on your own understanding; in all your ways acknowledge Him, and He will make your paths straight."

Respectful

Read Genesis 24:62-65.
Rebekah's respect for God naturally flowed into a respect for her husband. Two things happened that displayed this respectfulness upon seeing Isaac: 1) "She got down from her camel" (v. 64) and 2) "She took her veil and covered herself." (v. 65) In the movie *Braveheart*, a messenger approaches William Wallace (Mel Gibson) prior to the final battle. Before the messenger speaks, he gets off of his horse as a sign of respect. Rebekah does the same in a show of respect to Isaac. Ephesians 5:33 shows the depth of respect that's desired in a marriage relationship. "However, each one of you also must love his wife as he loves himself, and the wife must respect her husband."

Wow! How do you find a person like that? You become that person! Become the type of individual you would want to marry. If you are wishing for a prayer warrior, become a man of prayer. If you are looking for someone who knows the Word, let the Bible be your textbook. Christian speaker Gordon Banks says, "If you want something you've never had you've got to do something you've never done." The question is whether or not you are willing to go that far for a godly relationship. Look again at the wish list from Genesis 24. But this time put yourself to the test. See if you look like "The One" for her!

How do you measure up?

- In the Family
  - Do you know Christ as your personal Savior?
  - Are you allowing His forgiveness to move you past the mistakes you've made and shape you into a new creation?

- A Servant's Heart
  - How are you actively serving Jesus Christ?
  - How are you actively serving others?

- Trusting God
  - How do you respond when you are called from your comfort zone?
  - When Christ asks you to journey to a new place, is the response hesitation and procrastination or obedience?

- Respectful
  - Do you assert or submit your will to authority? (i.e. to parents, profs, and pastors)
  - Do you treat women with honor and respect or as the weaker sex?

Become the type of individual you would want to marry.

In order to find Ms. Right you have to first become Mr. Right. All too often, we become experts of picking out the faults of others while overlooking our own. "Why do you look at the speck of sawdust in your brother's eye and pay no attention to the plank in your own eye?" (Matt. 7:3). The responsibility of godliness first falls upon the man, so we must first put the wish list of a relationship upon ourselves. It isn't fair to wish for the characteristics of a godly girl, while refusing to seek the same in our own lives. Become the person you are wishing for and God will lead you to "The One."

Waiting

Read 1 Corinthians 7:32-34.

What is the purpose of being single?

How can He use you right where you are?

Waiting Sexually

We've heard this sermon so many times. But the ancient truth is still true and always will be. Waiting physically is something we know we should do. But why?

List four reasons why waiting sexually until marriage is important.

1.   3.
2.   4.

We often hear that we should wait, but I want to quickly address a few reasons why.

1. Consequences- There are consequences to sin. The consequences of premarital sex can be *spiritual*, (Our focus on Christ is affected), *physical* (pregnancy, disease) and *emotional* (heartache, low self-esteem, guilt, dependence on our partner).

2. Men and women view sex differently- Men respond to sex first physically then emotionally, while women respond first emotionally then physically. Therefore both are looking for something different. It has been said that men will use love to get sex and women will use sex to get love. If you took a survey on campus of why each gender desires physical intimacy, a stark contrast would surface. The men would answer because it feels good and the women would respond by saying they like to be held and feel secure. As a result, sex before marriage and even messing around, aren't seen through the same lens by both men and women.

3. Unmatched depth- Before marriage, the depth of physical intimacy is unmatched in the levels of emotional, spiritual, and conversational intimacy. The relationship is not sound enough to handle this closeness. Sex is an overflow of the emotional, spiritual, and conversational intimacy within marriage. I've always thought it interesting that society so often calls sex "making love" when the truth is sex should not be an attempt to create love but an avenue of expressing love that already exists.

4. Waiting communicates value and importance to the one you are waiting for- Saving yourself for marriage says to the one you marry, "You are important and worth any amount of sacrifice." Giving the gift of yourself is greater than the biggest engagement ring in a woman's eyes.

5. It's God's will- In 1 Thessalonians 4:3 it says, "It is God's will that you should be sanctified: that you should avoid sexual immorality." God has set parameters upon which life is to be lived and this is one of them. He is Creator and King so His Word can be trusted.

It would be foolish for me to assume that every guy reading this book is a virgin. Many of us have made mistakes in this area, but the good news is there's forgiveness. The grace of Christ can restore your virginity and give you a fresh start. We all have baggage. The question is, "Has the baggage been checked at the cross?" There are both godly men and women who have failed to wait. If it is a requirement for your wife to be a virgin, you will pass up many godly women. Her past is not as important as her future. Has the baggage for both of you been checked at the cross? Christ died for her sins too. He is in the restoration business for guys and girls.

Which reason for waiting on sex is a new concept to you and what are your thoughts about it?

What does this statement mean: "The grace of Christ can restore your virginity and give you a fresh start."

Actively Waiting

Waiting seems passive, but it can actually be very active. In my time of singleness I decided to actively wait on God instead of feeling sorry for myself.

- I began to pray for my wife before I ever knew her name. I would pray each day for her to grow in Christ and for God to remind her I was out there somewhere.
- I picked a star in the heavens for her and for me. In Genesis 15:5, God tells Abram that a star has been lit for each of his descendants, so I figured we each had one. When I'd look up and see our stars I'd pray and be encouraged that she was out there somewhere. To this day only Kelly and I know which two stars are ours.
- This one is going to surprise some of you, but I kept dating. Finding the right girl doesn't mean sitting in your dorm hoping for a knock on the door. Spending time with a girl **in a God honoring way** prepares you for the future. You will learn a ton about women and about yourself. And you might even have a little fun! It might be the right thing to discover she's the wrong one, and to have dated with God as the first priority. Comb your hair, brush your teeth, and go for it!
- The last aspect was in the form of notes. Not an email, but a good old fashioned love note. When I would think of "The One," I would just scribble a note to her on a napkin or piece of paper. I wrote to her over the course of seven years, sealing the envelope and placing the letter in a file. I wrote postcards on trips, during class in my notebook, and in a restaurant waiting to meet a friend—any time I had the urge to write, actively waiting. Here are some excerpts from my letters . . .

Dear ?,

" . . . I don't know if we've met or not. But I do know that I love you. It's so awesome that God has created us for each other. I don't know what's going on in your life right now but I'm praying for you . . ." (May 2, 1990)

Dear ?,

" . . . Waiting for you is difficult at times. I want God to bless me but I know it just isn't time . . . " (September 7, 1995; 12:33 a.m.)

Dear Kelly,

"This is the first note that I've written a name on. I believe that God has changed the ? to Kelly. WOW! I never thought the day would come. You are a gift from God and an answer to prayer. . ." (October 10, 1996; 5:19 p.m. on an American Airlines napkin between Dallas and Abilene)

Dear Kelly,

"This is the completion of my notes. Tomorrow, actually today we will be married . . ." (August 2, 1997; 2:41am) (2:41 *am! I guess I was a little nervous and couldn't fall asleep.*)

When we returned from our honeymoon I gave her a shoebox full of the notes written over the past seven years. Some "Dear ?" others "Dear Kelly." She sat and read each one and cried a bucket of tears. At times, I'll come home and find her with that shoebox in her lap reading them again. Actively waiting on Him builds our trust in the Lord and prepares us for the one He has for us.

What are some ways you can actively wait?

Take a moment and write a note to your future wife.

Encourage Your Group

1. Share how the diagnoses of the heart determine the direction.

2. Share the characteristic that needs to be added to your wish list. What needs to be removed or lowered in importance?

3. Examine the area you need to grow in to "become the person you want to marry."

4. Discuss the importance of waiting physically until marriage and how to achieve that goal.

Between You and God

1. Pray about your "want," declaring your want for Christ more than anything else.

2. Write a short prayer discussing your heart in the following areas of dating:

   Fear

   Hope

   Trusting God

   Waiting

3. Journal your thoughts on the aspect of dating in your life below:

Temptation: Winning the War
One Battle at a Time

Temptation: Winning the War One Battle at a Time

PAGE ONE—God creates the heavens and the earth.

PAGE TWO—Man is tempted and blows it. Temptation rears its head in Genesis and finally ceases in Revelation. Book by book, and account by account, one thing is indisputable when reading the stories of the Bible: Temptation is unavoidable in life. Just look at our lives today and think of the many vices that cry out for attention. We can't watch 30 minutes of prime time television, surf the Internet, or skim the pages of a popular magazine, and not have some piece of the world thrust in our face. The question is and always has been, how will we respond?

Name five temptations godly men face from popular culture today.

1.
2.
3.
4.
5.

The pages of the Bible are filled with responses, both good and bad, to many different forms of temptation. Check out this brief list of situations and the corresponding result of choices made for truth or error.

> **Sow a thought and you reap an act;**
> **Sow an act and you reap a habit;**
> **Sow a habit and you reap a character;**
> **Sow a character and you reap a destiny.**
> **—Anonymous**

- Don't listen to him. That's the wrong tree . . . **Fall of Man** (Gen. 3)
- Tell him she's your wife, not your sister, Abraham . . . **Fear** (Gen. 20)
- Goliath, humility is preferable to boasting . . . **Pride** (1 Sam. 17)
- David, don't take a second glance . . . **Adultery** (2 Sam. 11)
- Preach it, apostles; don't let the rulers quiet you . . . **Faith** (Acts 5:40,41)

Temptation is around us every day. It doesn't usually lurk in the bushes for a surprise attack. Instead, it slowly befriends us, convincing us that we have nothing to fear. "Don't worry, there's no harm," the world whispers. It's just a TV show or movie, just one beer, or just a small white lie. Each situation is justified until our perspective is a jaded edge of truth or no truth at all. In the process, we trade a foundation built on rock for a life centered on sand. How do we distinguish the truth from error in our world? And better yet, how do we battle temptation and look more like Jesus in the end?

Temptation: Its Origin and Destination

Imagine that it is the Friday afternoon before spring break. You and the guys are at the airport trying to get to the slopes. The snowboards and skis are reserved, the hotel is cheap but livable, and your boarding pass is in your hand. FAA rules require that the airline keep meticulous notes on where the plane is flying from and where it is going. On the TV screen it says it is coming from Baton Rouge and headed to Denver. But as you glance at the FAA form behind the check-in counter, you discover that is not the truth. Right there in black and white it says:

Origin: Louisiana junk yard
Destination: Side of Colorado mountain

What are you going to do?
[ ] Try your luck.
[ ] No way, José.
[ ] Don't worry, just have fun on the flight.
[ ] Call Greyhound.

Without hesitation, I'm passing on that vacation, thank you very much! It sounded like a great trip in the beginning, but once the true origin and destination were revealed, the trip lost its luster. No destination was going to be worth that price!

Read James 1:13-15.

Do these verses tell you . . .
• the origin of our temptation?   [ ] Yes   [ ] No   [ ] Not sure
• the destination of temptation? [ ] Yes   [ ] No   [ ] Not Sure

With an origin of evil desires and the destination being death, you would think the check-in counter for this ride would be empty. Instead, all too often we grip our boarding pass of temptation and dream of the pleasure on the opposite end. The quest might seem innocent for some; for others it may be premeditated, but for both the result is the same: Temptation brings sin and sin brings death! And to think . . . we were set up by our own desires. Enticed and dragged away by our choice, we become ". . . slaves to whatever has mastered us" (2 Pet. 2:19).

Why do you continue to board the airplane of sin, when you know the destination is death? Check the four that best describe you:

[ ] I like the way it feels.
[ ] It is a weak spot for me personally.
[ ] I got fooled initially, but now I'm addicted.
[ ] Other people do it all the time.
[ ] I haven't completely surrendered that area to God.
[ ] I lack any accountability on the issue.
[ ] I'm not the only one with this problem.
[ ] All of the above

Tackling Temptation

Write 1 Corinthians 10:13 in your own words below:

> "Truth is heavy, so few men carry it."
> —Jewish Proverb

In this verse Paul gives us the plan for making the godly decision. He acknowledges the existence of temptation and doesn't duck the fact that temptation is real and inevitable in each of our lives. But he also provides us some guidance on how to tackle temptation, and better yet, how to avoid it.

• The temptation is nothing new.
"No temptation has seized you except what is common to man" (1 Cor.10:13a).

The temptations you and I face are the same old tricks with a new coat of paint.

Let's compare two time periods and identify the new paint of our day. In the lists below, match the sin on the left with the Old West example on the right.

Today's Sin	The Old West
a. Materialism	___ "I've got the biggest ranch in town."
b. Cheating	___ Train robbery at sundown
c. Lust	___ Mighty nice gun
d. Greed	___ An extra ace in the deck
e. Pride	___ Saloon girls

39

God's Response to Temptation

1) The fork in the road . . .

"The world and its desires pass away, but the man who does the will of God lives forever" (1 John 2:17).

Temptation presents each man with a fork in the road and a choice to make. Which way do I go? One path builds character; the other tears it down. The street signs may read "Integrity Avenue" and "Pornography Lane," or they may be "Truth Road" and "Lies Circle." It has been said, "Choice not chance determines destiny." Our life is shaped by choices we make with none bigger than the decision to trust God at the fork of temptation.

2) You are not alone . . .

"And God is faithful; he will not let you be tempted beyond what you can bear" (1 Cor. 10:13b).

Satan wants nothing more than for you to feel isolated in temptation. Like Eve in the garden of Eden or Jesus in the desert, Satan tries to get us in the corner and bully us into a wrong choice. He is the great tempter, coming in many forms, and whispering in just the right voice. But hear this: **You are not alone.** Men throughout history and even those walking around your campus today have been faced with similar temptations and proved victorious. And better yet, all of heaven is standing on your side. The Bible mentions "a great cloud of witnesses" (Heb. 12:1), who are urging you on against the struggles that are "common to man." Be encouraged; you are not alone when temptation knocks on your heart. You are flanked on every side by the Holy Spirit of God. Calling upon Him will crush any enemy and set your feet on the path of life.

3) Faithfulness

"If we are faithless, he will remain faithful, for he cannot disown himself" (2 Tim. 2:13).

"The one who calls you is faithful and he will do it" (1 Thess. 5:24).

"He is faithful" means that God is right there every step of the way. God is not a ruthless professor wanting to give us pop quizzes of temptations, but a loving God who's already given the answer to the test—the cross. Jesus can be nothing but faithful because His whole life from birth to death was an act of faith for you and me.

4) Provides strength

"So I say, live by the Spirit, and you will not gratify the desires of the sinful nature" (Gal. 5:16).

Temptation will never be more than we can handle when we are looking to the Spirit and not our flesh for strength. Our will power, no matter how determined, and our flesh, no matter how good, will always make the wrong decision at a point of weakness. Only the Spirit of God is stronger than the cries of our sinful nature. Only when the old man is defeated and the Spirit resides in us can temptation be managed and victory be won.

How can we find strength in His faithfulness during temptation?

Why does it feel like some temptations are more than you can bear?
    [ ] I'm trusting in my flesh and not His Spirit to carry me.
    [ ] I'm looking at the problem, not the solution.
    [ ] I'm not daily growing in Christ, so I am very weak in my choices.
    [ ] All I see are the short term benefits and not the long term consequences.

5) Provides an escape, a way out

" . . . He will also provide a way out so that you can stand up under it" (1 Cor. 10:13c).

Finally, the last statement of verse 13 reveals a way out. In every temptation there is an escape hatch. Just as Joseph avoided sin with Potiphar's wife in Genesis 39, we must choose a similar response: **Turn and run.** The escape routes don't come easy because they usually require two phases of discernment: 1) We have to say no to the desires of our flesh and yes to Christ, and 2) We have to take a stand (and that may mean run). Doing an about face and running the opposite direction may mean . . .
    • changing the channel
    • leaving the party
    • clicking off the Internet
    • driving her home
    • keeping our eyes on our own paper

41

> ## "The world needs men and women . . . who can say no with emphasis, although the rest of the world says yes.
> —Chuck Swindoll

My escape hatch – Saying "no" and making a "stand"

I own a scar-filled testimony of being the high school party animal and then coming to Christ. Before I placed my faith in Jesus I partied with my friends each weekend. With only two Christian friends— Kim and Russell—and an army of lost ones, I had some major temptations to handle. Friday nights as a young Christian were tough, and one of my first escape hatches was choosing to drink soda at the party. Someone would ask if I'd like a beer and I'd say, "No thanks; I already have a drink. I'm driving tonight," or "Bro, I'm on a caffeine high." Slowly, the temptation of fitting in with the crowd faded and my friends would honor my effort by putting sodas in the ice chest for me. Choosing this escape route enabled me to share Christ with many of my lost friends. Some trusted Him, some just listened and others thought I was crazy (and still do). The soda enabled me to make a stand. Over time, God led me to another escape route: to quit going to the parties all together and look for other opportunities to hang out with those friends. The escape moved from changing drinks to changing venues. Either way, Christ's leadership drew me closer to Him.

What are some escape hatches in the following scenarios?

Scenario: "Everybody" is headed to a bar and you know that is a tough place for you to live out God's plan.

Escape Hatch:

Scenario: The homework is due in two hours; your page is blank and your friend's is completed. He's encouraging you to copy away.

Escape Hatch:

Remove the Logs

You are going to think I'm kidding, but it's true—My wife's hometown is Comfort, Texas. It is a small town in the Texas hill country, full of great people and beautiful scenery. Often the entire family will have a campfire on the ranch. S'mores, hot chocolate, and roasted hot dogs are the typical gourmet menu. Throughout the evening we keep the blaze alive by placing logs and branches into the flames. Being a closet pyromaniac, I enjoy adding logs to the blaze. More wood means more fire. When the night begins to wind down we don't put any more wood in the fire. Less wood means less fire.

Controlling the blaze of sin and temptation is no different. Instead of trying to extinguish the fire when it is raging, we must stop feeding it. For example, during college the Lord revealed to me (particularly in the area of lust), that I needed to remove the logs if the flames were going to decrease. I couldn't have posters of girls on the walls, watch MTV all day, and see every movie that came out then expect my lust to subside. I realized that the second glances on campus and the images my eyes were allowed to ingest

were just putting another log on the fire. The saying is true, "Garbage in. Garbage out."
Read Psalm 101: 2,3.

Fill in the blanks: (v. 2) "I will be careful to lead a _____ _____—
...I will walk in my house with _____ _____. (v. 3) I will set before
my _____ no vile thing."

What area of temptation is your greatest struggle? Check the appropriate box below.
[ ] Pride
[ ] Lust
[ ] Materialism
[ ] Anger
[ ] Other_____
                (Please specify)

What logs do you need to remove in order to stand firm in this temptation?

A Man's ~~Best~~ Worst Friend

Let's look specifically at an area of temptation that haunts most college men: sexual lust.
Every man knows the struggle this brings to our Christian walk and would agree it's a
daily battle. You are walking across campus, thinking of a project that is due and then
she walks by. WHAM! The thoughts race downhill like a roller coaster, and in a mil-
lisecond we're toast. The clothes girls wear (or don't wear these days), the commercials
and TV shows, the magazine rack, the Internet, and the 15 seconds that make the R
rating all prey on the purity of a godly man's mind. I can remember praising God for
winter so the girls on campus would put some clothes on. Is it really possible to honor
God sometime this millennium? Or should we just put up the white flag and concede?

Read Proverbs 5:1-10.

Describe the adulterous woman in verses 3-6.

Show the lie lust tells in these verses.

> "The things
> that play in the
> theater of our mind will
> shape our heart
> and actions."
> —Bob DeMoss

Look again at Proverbs 5:8 and fill in the blanks:

"Keep to a path _____ from her, _____ _____ go near the door of her house."

This verse is a log remover for us. Stay far away it says; walk on the other side of the street, because you are playing with fire. Here's the honest truth of this verse: Don't just say no to the rooms in the house; say no to the doorstep. Don't even get close! The problem is that we love the door, taking temptation to its outer limit. "It's outside the house," we reason, "barely on her property. What can a knock on the door hurt?"

The Lie: Standing on the porch giving a gentle knock is innocent.
The Truth: The door is the beginning point of a deadly visit.

We are never satisfied with just a knock! Each time we feed our lust, it takes us to the next level. The spiral quickly twirls downward until the need for satisfaction leads us on a tour of the house. Guilt quickly slams the door on our desire and we wind up back on the front porch guilty of trespassing once again. It's a vicious cycle for a man unless the door is defined and our hormones are placed in Christ's control. In order to keep lust from digging our graves, we must define and confront this problem in our lives.

Define the door to lust for you.
   [ ] Entertaining thoughts
   [ ] Second glances and wandering eyes
   [ ] A mouse click on www . . .
   [ ] TV and movies
   [ ] Magazines

What three words describe your feelings when you return to the doorstep after a tour of the house?
   1.
   2.
   3.

Continue reading Proverbs 5:7-14.

List some of the results of unchecked passions:
   1.
   2.
   3.

Winning the Next Battle

As in any war, the offensive must be strategic and logical. Therefore, let's look at the attack plan for conquering temptation from four different fronts. Applying these things will help you discover the victory that is in Christ.

1) Look away

"I made a covenant with my eyes not to look lustfully at a girl" (Job 31:1).
"Do not lust in your heart after her beauty" (Prov. 6:25).
Walking away from the door means we must turn our head and look the other way. If that's unavoidable, then our best defense may just be to close our eyes. Refusing the glance or the second look that triggers our thoughts is the key. I have investigated the concrete of many sidewalks as a girl has passed me on the way to class. It is fine to appreciate the beauty God has created, but when lustful looks turn to lustful thoughts, it's difficult to defuse a ticking bomb.

During the Christmas break of my freshman year, my high school friends were all home from college, so we decided to hang out. Craig, who attended The Naval Academy, had no interest in the video games we were playing. He just turned the other way and flipped through a magazine talking with the guys. Finally, after offering my controller to him countless times, I asked what the deal was. His response was simple but profound, "My goal is to be a Navy pilot and they must have perfect vision. Video games could hurt my eyes." Craig's focus was on something greater than a temporary satisfaction. Ours should be too. If we want to conquer sexual lust we must first choose to look away from that which could hold us back, making a covenant of purity with our eyes!

2) Read and know the Word

"For these commands are a lamp, this teaching is a light, and the corrections of discipline are the way to life, keeping you from the immoral woman, from the smooth tongue of the wayward wife" (Prov. 6:23).

Put the above verse into your own words:

> "You can't stop a bird from flying in front of your face, but you can stop it from making a nest on your head."
> —Chinese proverb

What are ways I can make the Bible a part of my life?

What are the benefits of my reading and knowing the Word? Here are just a few:

A) The Word arms us for battle. Ephesians 6:13-17 details the full armor of God. Each aspect is vital to our defense against any temptation, but only one provides offense against evil: "the sword of the Spirit, which is the Word of God" (v. 17).

B) The Word is the opposite of death. "For the word of God is living and active" (Heb. 4:12). Make no mistake, when you read the Bible you are reading about life. And life is contrary to the death we find in sexual lust or any sin.

C) The Word is a filter for the filth. "It judges the thoughts and attitudes of the heart. Nothing in all creation is hidden from God's sight" (Heb. 4:12,13). So often, lust is a mask we hide behind and a masquerade we play with God. We can't avoid the verses that cut straight to the bone, and this is one of them. God sees everything!

D) The Word is undefeatable and indisputable when spoken. In the three recorded temptations in Luke 4:1-13, Jesus combated Satan each time by quoting the book of Deuteronomy. It was one-on-one for 40 days in the desert . . . and the Word won! Proverbs 30:5,6 says, "Every word of God is flawless . . . do not add to His words."

Do you see the value of His Word? Ingesting the Word of God brings delight to life, but more importantly, it covers our lives in the very name of God. We no longer walk into temptation alone but carry the banner of His name across our lives.

- Start reading the book of John, Philippians, Proverbs or Psalms.
- Do a weekly Bible study (alone or in a group).
- Keep a journal of what you read.
- Meditate on a verse of your choice each day.
- Write a verse on a note card and recite it throughout the day.
- Memorize your favorite verses.
- Listen to talks on tape or radio.

List three ways in which reading the Bible can help you handle temptation.
1.
2.
3.

Find a verse from this section on temptation and memorize it this week. Write your verse on a separate piece of paper and carry it with you in your wallet.

3) Identify your weak moments

"When the devil had finished all this tempting, he left him until an opportune time" (Luke 4:13).

The temptation of Christ ends with two powerful words: opportune time. The devil left Jesus this time, but his sights were set upon a strategic return. Satan knows our weak moments and wants to use them to his advantage. He is patient also and will wait until the right time to tempt us in the wrong place. Each one of us has chinks in our spiritual armor. For some it is the computer, while for others it is TV. When we recognize the slippery places in our lives, we are a step closer to stopping the fall, and another log is removed from the fire.

Let me give you a personal example. A few years ago I realized television was a weak point for me. I would flip through the stations and just veg, wasting time, no real harm in it. Late at night it would turn dangerous, as my watching would give birth to lustful thoughts. The shows were different and my guard was down. One night I even watched the Spanish speaking channel until it dawned on me that I don't speak Spanish! But that actress sure was cute. Now I have made a rule: No channel surfing after midnight. The clock strikes twelve and the power (escape hatch) button is pressed. Identifying the chink in my armor and guarding it helped me move forward.

What are some of your weak moments in the area of lust (or another temptation)?

> "He who does not want to fall should not walk in slippery places."
> —Ancient Proverb

4) Fight on your knees

• Prayer is a great defense against sexual sin. When we cry out to God for help, He will answer. When faced with temptation, take it to Him in prayer. Pray for His strength to be your strength and for Him to reveal a means of escape. You can't get knocked down if you are already on your knees.

"Set your mind on things above, not on earthly things" (Col. 3:2).

• Pray for the girl that is the object of your lust. "Pray for her? What in the world are you talking about?" Whenever my thoughts begin to head down the tubes, I pray for the girl. I pray for her relationship with Christ, either for it to begin or to grow. I pray for God to provide her a godly man or to spiritually strengthen the husband she may already have. I've found when the prayers start, the lust ends. She is now a person instead of an object of infatuation. Whether the girl is an actress or a classmate, prayer can change your thoughts and also bless her life.

Jot down two ways in which praying for a girl can change your thoughts about her.

1.
2.

List three things you could pray for her below.

1.
2.
3.

When Right Intentions Go Wrong

At times we are going to look temptation eye to eye and give in. It happens to all of us. But the grace of Jesus is stronger than our weakness. When we blow it, we should confess it and move on. Don't try to shuffle it under the rug, pay it back with a good deed, or plead for an installment of forgiveness. If you are a born again believer, you are the righteousness of Christ and have already received all the forgiveness of the cross.

The apostle Paul spoke of struggling with sin in Romans 7, but that wasn't the domino that triggered a lifestyle of sin. He might have had right intentions go wrong, but His identity was still in Jesus. Paul was like any other Christian, a sinner by nature but changed into a saint by the grace of God. It's this radical forgiveness afforded by the blood of Jesus that gives us a grasp of the Lord's words in 2 Corinthians 12:9: "My grace is sufficient for you, for my power is made perfect in weakness." And Paul's response gives us hope when temptation is near. "Therefore I will boast all the more gladly about my weaknesses, so that Christ's power may rest on me. . . . For when I am weak, then I am strong" (2 Cor. 12: 9,10).

"God is more concerned with our character than our comfort. His goal is not to pamper us physically but to perfect us spiritually."
—Paul W. Powell

the highest education:
becoming a godly man

Encourage Your Group

1. As a group, come up with a definition of temptation.

2. Discuss your plan for standing in the midst of temptation.

3. Choose an accountability partner for next week. Fill in the blanks and exchange your answers with him.

   • My biggest temptation is _____.
   • Here are two ways you can pray for me:
       1.
       2.
   • Hold me accountable and encourage me by:
       [ ] A phone call
       [ ] An email
       [ ] Pray for me daily
       [ ] Ask me the following question when you see me.
           (Write the question below.)

Between You and God

1. Thank God for His forgiveness through Christ.

2. Lay before Him your greatest temptation.

3. Ask the Holy Spirit to show you:
       a) the chinks in your armor
       b) an escape route
       c) the resource of Christ in your heart

Money: Managing the Lint in your Pocket

Money: Managing the Lint in your Pocket

"A chapter on money? Why in the world would I need to hear about that? First of all, I wish I had some money to be worried about and second, it's too soon for me to be thinking about my current or future financial status." Well, it's true that most college guys have more change underneath their couch cushions than in their pockets. And, managing the lint in those pockets is a better description of college finances than actual money management. But the topic of money is one that can't be overlooked or avoided if you are to be a godly man. Money issues are all around you. From school loans to credit cards, date nights to gas in the car, most of us at some point have either inherited or conditioned ourselves to the world's view or God's view on money.

Take a look at this story and see what I mean.

A Chicago radio station had a contest for the "craziest thing you would do" for a prize of $10,000. Of the 6,000 applicants, a male college student won! A sophomore from Indiana State University named Jay said he would eat an 11-foot birch tree for the ten grand. So, dressed in a tuxedo with pruning sheers in hand, at a table of fine china and linen tablecloth, Jay bellied up to the task. Lucky for him, he got to choose one condiment to swallow it down with . . . just one.

What condiment would you have chosen?
[ ] French Dressing   [ ] Thousand Island   [ ] Ranch
[ ] Mustard   [ ] Ketchup
[ ] Or write in your choice _____

He chose French dressing (YUCK!) then began to clip and eat. Inch by inch, he ate it all. Leaves, branches, trunk, bark, roots, the entire 11-foot tree! Three days and 18 hours of actual eating time later and the $10,000 was his. (*Campus Life*, December 1980, p. 19.)

What's the craziest thing you would do for $10,000?

What response best describes your reaction to this story:
    [ ] "There's no way. That guy is nuts."
    [ ] "I can top that. Just show me the money."

This story shows how our world—and especially men—view money. In general, men are motivated and sometimes driven by a quest for cash, to the point that sometimes a loss of reality accompanies our desire for more. Whether it's via a "How crazy can you be?" contest or something more realistic like earning a graduate degree or taking on a side job, we are constantly bombarded with a desire to earn more, get the most, or provide what will be needed to make it in life. This can be a real risk-or-reward proposition. It is crucial to realize now your strengths and weaknesses with money issues and to hear what God has to say on this subject. Don't wait until your post-college days to brush off the bad habits. Address the issue now before graduation and let God free your financial future. You can be obtaining the highest education as you learn to manage the change in your pocket.

Why does the college man need this information?
- There are around 2000 verses in the Bible on the subject of finances and possessions. Jesus spoke more about money than judgement, communion, baptism, the Word of God and the second coming. (Promise Keepers Pamphlet "5 Steps to Financial Freedom")
- Of Americans, 80 percent owe more than they own. (Promise Keepers Pamphlet "5 Steps to Financial Freedom")
- Of all divorces, 56 percent are the result of financial issues in marriage.
- Only 17 percent of *Christian* adults claim to tithe regularly, and only 3 percent actually tithe.

Why do you think Jesus mentioned finances so frequently?

Read Mark 8:36 and write down what it says.

Society's Influence

Andrew Carnegie, a millionaire in the early 1900s, was asked, "How much money does it take to make a man happy?" His answer is still a reality today: "A dollar more."

During the 1998 NBA strike, Patrick Ewing of the New York Knicks, who was making $18 million a year, was quoted as saying, "It's about survival, about being able to feed our families." ("Sports Desk," *New York Times*, 29 October 1998, sec. D, p.1.)

Those testimonies are from men who have no need for more, yet happiness is still another dollar away. Is that you? Maybe we can't relate to the $18 million per year or even fathom the wealth of Carnegie, but in our hearts we still struggle with the same temptation. Just one look at our wardrobe, our car, our sunglasses, or our shoes and we can't help but notice the standard our world sets for us.

In what ways does our society love money?

"There are three conversions necessary: the conversion of the heart, mind, and purse."
—Martin Luther

In what ways do you love money?

Why do we love money? That's the question we must ask ourselves. Is it simply for the look of a name brand shirt, the feel of leather interior, or the sound of *Star Wars* on surround sound? No, we're smart enough to know that styles come and go and our tastes change. We love money simply for the approval, self-esteem, and value it brings. It makes us important; it provides an outlet; and it touches our competitive spirit and desire to win. Money quenches our ego for a moment, but leaves us thirsty for more. Just like Carnegie and Ewing, more is all we need!

This attitude birthed by society is a contradiction to what the Word of God has to say about money. Here are some examples: 1) Read 1 Timothy 6:7-10. 2) Ecclesiastes 5:10 says, "Whoever loves money never has money enough; whoever loves wealth is never satisfied with his income." 3) Matthew 6:19-21 adds, "Do not store up for yourselves treasures on earth, where moth and rust destroy, and where thieves break in and steal. But store up for yourselves treasures in heaven, . . . For where your treasure is, there your heart will be also."

What are the truths you find in these passages to guide you in becoming a godly man?
    1.
    2.
    3.

Trusting Jesus for provision is not a vow of poverty for the Christian, but a declaration of intent for our lives. That intent is placing Christ first in all things despite the allure of worldly gain. From the $1.50 it takes to buy Starbucks to the thousands of dollars we invest in a pentium processor, each dollar spent in attaining a piece of this world is not a replacement for what God wants to do in our lives. He is never plan-B in times of need. He is all we need!

Read Luke 18:18-25.

Think about the rich young ruler in these verses. He wanted something money can't buy—eternal life. Jesus' answer was unpopular, "Sell everything you have . . ." OUCH! "When he heard this he became very sad, because he was a man of great wealth" (v. 23). What was Jesus' intent? To ban all rich people from His team? No. To punish all smart, talented young men who are climbing the ladder of success? No. It was simply a challenge to the intent of the young ruler's heart. His attitude was lifestyle first, eternal life second. But the offer of Jesus was just the opposite. Money couldn't buy eternity then, and it still can't today!

College is full of men who crave a business card that will read "Rich, Young, Ruler" and the lifestyle it produces. "I have money to burn, time ahead, and I'm the man!" We stare anxiously at a ladder to climb after graduation and the security we'll have with each step to the top. Yet we forget our only true security is found in one man—Jesus Christ!

From the view of television advertisers, check three results of money from the list below that you think would best sell to college men.

[ ] success
[ ] attractiveness to girls
[ ] prestige
[ ] good looks
[ ] security
[ ] power
[ ] plenty of toys

Your Family's Influence

Can you remember the first time you held a dollar bill or heard money mentioned? I can't. It was so early in life that my long-term memory was yet to exist. It might have been in the delivery room as the doctor told my dad how much the bundle of joy cost him! From piggy banks to allowances, lawn-mowing jobs to birthday money, our familiarity with dollars and cents begins at a young age. It's unavoidable. Even in our adolescent years we are inundated with the worth and meaning of money.

My wife Kelly teaches kindergarten, and since we don't have any kids of our own, each day of school is parenting practice for her. One day she was having the kids do an activity using play money to teach them the value of the dollar. As Kelly distributed the phony cash, she noticed a little five-year-old girl throwing her money in the air. As the money fell around her she sang the popular chorus, "Money, Money, Money . . . MON-ey." Five years old and already love struck by the almighty dollar. Where was this learned? At that age, it was most likely learned at **home**.

In what ways did you learn about money from your family?

Notice the good or bad in these situations, and see if any remind you of your family:
- Dad throws a fit over the costs of repairing the car.
- Dad comes to town on business and takes you and your roommates to dinner.
- Your parents are buying a new house, while you take out a new school loan.
- Parents call a family meeting before each month to pray over what to give.
- Parents spend $30 per ticket on a pro football game and put $1 in the offering plate.
- Mom trades in a career to take care of the kids.

Without even knowing it, our habits and view of money may be the product of a long line of family members who have treated money in similar fashion. Like the branches on a family tree, the lineage of good or bad financial stewardship can continue or end with you. In a 400-meter relay, the anchor leg of the race is at the mercy of the previous three runners. But upon the transfer of the baton into his hands, he becomes responsible. It is up to the person holding the baton to run the best race possible. If your parents have been faithful with money, consider yourself blessed and follow in their steps. If your parents have been foolish with money, as the baton is passed, run at a new pace. Don't settle for less. Run a smart race so that when your turn comes for a hand off, financial wisdom will be the legacy.

Does this make you want to become a godly man? [ ] Yes   [ ] No   [ ] Confused

My family's greatest weakness in dealing with money is: (Check all that apply)
    [ ] Debt is taking its toll.
    [ ] Our identity is in money.
    [ ] We hold on and never give.
    [ ] We're cheapskates; we never spend.
    [ ] If we have it, we spend it.
    [ ] We've never planned for the future.
    [ ] We buy what we don't need.

My family's greatest strength in dealing with money is: (Check all that apply)
    [ ] Giving is a joy.
    [ ] We've made good investments.
    [ ] We're hard-working, doing the best we can.
    [ ] We've made much out of little.
    [ ] We know how to save.
    [ ] We spend wisely and enjoy life.
    [ ] Kids prospered while parents sacrificed.
    [ ] Prayer is the first step to purchase.

How has your upbringing influenced you in the area of finances? Jot down some thoughts.

    Positively:

    Negatively:

> "A person who has been a Christian for even a short while can fake prayer, Bible study, evangelism, and going to church, but he can't fake what his checkbook reveals."
> —Ron Blue

A Practical Look at Your Money

In the previous sections, we have addressed the different ways money affects us all. Over the remainder of this chapter we want to deal in a practical sense with your money as a college student. We will look at three areas: **debt, savings** and **giving**. In each of these areas, we need some practical teaching and godly wisdom. Prior to each section there will be an opportunity for you to assess your personal situation in a question or fill-in-the-blank format.

debt n. 1: That which is owed 2: An obligation to make payment in money or goods and services
- My unpaid credit card balance is $_____.
- I still owe $_____ on my car.
- I still owe $_____ on _____.
- My student loans today are $_____ and by the time I plan to graduate they will be $_____.
- Putting this all together, my total debt today is $_____, and by the time I graduate will be $_____.
- The primary reason I'm in debt is:
    - [ ] Credit Cards
    - [ ] Student Loans
    - [ ] Buying stuff I don't need
    - [ ] Valid reasons beyond my control
    - [ ] "I HAVE NO DEBT"

Necessary vs. Unnecessary Debt

For college students there are essentially two types of debt: necessary and unnecessary. Necessary debt, for the sake of this chapter, will be debt you can't avoid at this point of your life. Unnecessary debt will be debt you absolutely can live without.

Necessary Debt

For the college student, the main source of necessary debt is school loans. This is a necessary debt because college is an investment in your future and for many reasons is a blessing.

Here are a few of these blessings:
- Allows you to receive opportunities that might otherwise not have happened
- Makes you a more attractive hire
- Increases your earning potential
- Proves you can conquer a challenge

Basically, your loans are seeds that will be paid back at harvest, and there should be no delay in your willingness to pay the loans off. Just because the interest rate is low, don't use that as a crutch and postpone debt repayment.

Now, if you are fortunate enough to have parents pay for the school loans or can afford school outright, don't take it for granted. Take time today or this week to thank your folks for the debt they have assumed on your behalf. That is money in your pocket after graduation.

Unnecessary Debt

While student loans are a down payment on a future career, the main source of unnecessary debt is the credit card. Whether our parents give us one for emergencies, we sign up for one on a whim in the campus center, or we just like the feel of having money at our disposal, credit cards can be a dangerous outlet if used without restraint. They are so dangerous that many college students dig themselves a hole that will take years to crawl out of. That debt is the noose around their neck. The deception for the college student is that it often doesn't become taut until graduation.

Take a guess at what the average American family's credit card balance is:
- [ ] $500
- [ ] $2,000
- [ ] $7,500
- [ ] $12,500
- [ ] $15,000

The winner—or actually the loser—is (drum roll please) . . . $12,500. (Rick Beggs Ronald Blue & Co. 1997) Amazing isn't it? And this was in 1997. It's much higher now! Let's take a look at how the credit card works.

Median Earnings for Persons 18 or Older by Educational Attainment:

No high school diploma	$17,148
High school graduate	$22,502
Some college, no degree	$26,090
Associate degree	$29,457
Bachelor's degree	$36,525
Master's degree	$45,053
Professional degree	$65,916
Doctorate	$56,758

U.S. Bureau of the Census, 1997 (www.collegeplan.org)

Suppose you buy a computer for $1,000 on your credit card, and you pay the basic minimum each month of about $20 at a normal interest rate of 18 percent. It will take you roughly seven years to pay it off. When you finally do pay it off, it will have cost you $1,803.95. The bottom line is that credit card companies allow interest to work for them. As a result, an innocent purchase can become a black hole.

Credit cards are the temptation and debt is the trap. "People who want to get rich fall into temptation and a trap and into many foolish and harmful desires that plunge men into ruin and destruction" (1 Tim. 6:9).

unnecessary debt

Listen to the testimony of one college student.

" . . . I am embarrassed to admit to you that I have so much debt on my credit card ($20,000). I held off getting one because I had heard stories. Then someone advised me to build my credit history with a credit card and only use it to buy groceries. Well, it started out as a good cause and then I 'needed' this and 'had to have' that and now I am paying for most of what I can't even remember getting."

Take time to read Romans 13:8 and write down what it says below.

Here's the cold hard truth: if you do not pay off your credit cards every single month, you need to quit using them. It may be helpful to have some plastic handy for that flat tire or sudden emergency, but if that emergency becomes a new shirt or dinner for your date, keep the card in your wallet. That's the most practical advice I can give you. Creditors have little concern for the victims affected by one person's mistakes. Not only do you pay for your credit history, but potentially a spouse or children are also affected.

If this chapter on money is a day late and a dollar short, and debt is already a fixture of monthly statements, let me give you some spiritual direction and practical application for your life:

For your heart
1. Pray – Ask God to break you of poor spending habits.
2. Surrender – Give God full control over your financial situation.

For your wallet
1. Stop going into debt – Quit buying the frivolous stuff. The hole just gets deeper.
2. Start paying off debt – Put every nickel toward the balance. The greater the commitment, the sooner you're free.

Some college administrators have realized the danger credit card solicitors bring to college students and have banned them from their schools.
—USA TODAY,
March 12, 1999

the highest education:
becoming a godly man

saving v. 1: to put aside money for the future

My biggest difficulty in saving is:
- [ ] Being disciplined
- [ ] I can't make the bills and save
- [ ] I don't see the value

Okay, here's where this chapter crosses the line for a college student. I know what you're thinking: "I don't even have money to spend, much less save." It says in Proverbs 13:11, "He who gathers money little by little makes it grow." Saving isn't fun and has very few short-term rewards. It's a habit that takes discipline and long-term thinking, and just by the nature of that equation many folks don't make the effort to save. Proof of that fact was in an alarming statistic by the Social Security Administration that shows 85 percent of Americans by the age of 65 have less than $250 in savings. (Ron Blue, *Master Your Money*) Now, compare that amount with the $12,500 credit card debt and . . . "Houston, we have a problem."

"In the house of the wise are stores of choice food and oil, but a foolish man devours all he has" (Prov. 21:20).

Saving money in college is difficult without question. It doesn't seem to add up to much, so why do it? The importance of saving now is to develop habits for the future as well as to prepare for what lies ahead. If you learn now to sacrifice immediate wants for future needs you will be ahead of the game. This is an area in which my family has had a positive influence in my life. As a result, I realized the value of saving throughout college. Saving a little money here and there enabled me to go on the ski trip during spring break, to purchase a special present, to handle an unexpected expense, and to give to a friend in need. Starting with just a little bit each month will develop into a discipline that will last a lifetime. Take my word for it, life is going to get more expensive the older you get, *so start good habits now.*

What's a small sacrifice you can make in order to save? (Check all that apply)
- [ ] Eat out less
- [ ] Buy fewer cd's
- [ ] No new clothes
- [ ] Cancel cable TV or newspaper
- [ ] Other _____

> **Check this out:**
> If you were to save $1,000 a year, which is about $83/month or $2.68/day, and you were to put that in some type of investment earning 12.5 percent for 40 years, at the end of that time you would have turned $40,000 into $1,000,000.

Set a goal for yourself right now, and post a reminder of that goal somewhere you will see it every day.

"I'm going to save $_____ each month."

giving v. 1: Bestow, make a present of; donate

- Giving money away is:
    - [ ] crazy
    - [ ] a joy
    - [ ] an obligation
- If I had the salary of a NBA star, the first place I would give is _____.
- When it comes to supporting my church . . .
    - [ ] Don't ask.
    - [ ] I give regularly.
    - [ ] I know I should but I don't.
    - [ ] They have plenty—you should see the pastor's house.

The third area is the area of giving. Why give? I mean, we've earned this money right? It's ours isn't it? Well, two reasons give importance to this topic.

1) When we give, we release the grip money has on us and the grip we have on it.

Whether it's through a donation to the church, supporting a missionary or buying a friend's lunch, we are freed from the grip of money. This may make no financial sense, but it honors God. It's His anyway! Psalm 24:1 says, "The earth is the Lord's and everything in it, the world and all who live in it." We must be good stewards of that which has been given to us. One of the humbling truths of God's Word is no matter how hard we work or how much we think we deserve it, our money is God's. Letting go, then, is releasing what is already His.

- The loan money . . . it's His!
- The extra cash from work . . . it's His!
- The check from mom and dad . . . it's His!

Write out Psalm 24:1.

What is a significant point made by David in this verse?

2) When we give, it touches eternity!

Our resources can touch lives and make an impact in the kingdom of God. Your willingness to open your wallet in love can broaden a ministry, help a friend, and support the leadership of a church or organization. It may take some sacrifice, but it furthers His plans and touches others for an eternity. You do not have to give a lot to make a difference. Often we procrastinate in giving by saying, "Lord, once I'm rich, then I will give a whole lot." A quick read of John 6, the story of the boy with five loaves and two fish, and the two pennies of the widow in Luke 21, and it's quick to see that Jesus can multiply the gifts of the heart.

How much should I give?

There is much debate over what percentage of our income God wants us to give. Is it a strict 10 percent or is there freedom to choose? In the Old Testament we read about the "tithe," defined as a "tenth." The New Testament, on the other hand, speaks more about the position of our heart (2 Cor. 8,9) and setting aside a portion of income (1 Cor. 16:1,2). Since we as Christians have the Holy Spirit indwelling our lives, His leadership will be made known as we seek Him. Often in our faith we prefer to set parameters instead of embracing freedom in Christ. "If there is a specific rule just let me know and I'll do it." This removes the challenge of seeking Him and listening to the Spirit.

So what can we make of all this?
- We are to set aside a portion of our income on a regular basis.
- We are not bound to 10 percent. We are to seek Jesus in our giving decisions. God may call some to give 20 percent.
- There is freedom in Christ as we help financially to build His kingdom.

Write 2 Corinthians 9:6-8 in your own words below:

Number from 1-3, the areas which need the most improvement in your life, with 1 being the area needing the most improvement:
- ___ debt
- ___ savings
- ___ giving

> "Frankly, it was discouraging for me as a CPA to prepare income tax returns several years ago for my Christian friends and to discover they were giving practically nothing to their church and charities."
>
> **Rod Handley,**
> **CFO of FCA,**
> *Character Counts*

What's the answer?

The answer is found in 1 Timothy 6:11.

Verse 11 is the final bow on the issue of finances. Don't seek more money, but seek more of God. The "more" we want is righteousness, godliness, faith, love, perseverance and gentleness. This will honor God. In seeking the highest education, these are important words to help you become a godly man.

A couple of years ago my faith was put to the test when Breakaway, the ministry I lead, discovered there was only $76 left in the account at semester's end. Our expenses, on the other hand, were $8,000 per month and we didn't have 1 percent of that in the bank. What did we do? Well, we didn't try to drum up support. We got on our faces and went to God. We trusted God's call to this ministry and believed He would be a God of the 9th inning in our trial. In the next three weeks, $22,000 in donations were mailed in, with the majority being individual gifts of less than $100. It brought to life Matthew 6:33, "Seek first His kingdom and his righteousness, and all these things will be given to you as well." It also validated our philosophy on finances: "If we do God's things, He'll pay for them."

The real question for you and me is are we willing to surrender to God's plan for our finances instead of the world's. "You cannot serve both God and money" (Matt. 6:24). We must cross the line and make a choice. It's not a vow of poverty. It's not restricting your success and drive to be the best. It's simply adjusting the focus and intent of your heart. Is your focus to be a godly man? God has promised to meet all your needs (Phil. 4:19). Trust Him and He will provide.

Encourage Your Group

1. Discuss: If I won a million bucks tomorrow, the first three things I'd do would be . . .
   1.
   2.
   3.

2. Share why most men seem to love money. How does the love of money reveal itself in your life?

3. Emphasize how society's view of money affects you. What about your family's view of money? List some of the effects with another Christian.

4. Why, in your opinion, did Jesus mention our relationship with finances so often?

5. Share how a godly man stays free from the love of money.

6. Guys, I need you to hold me financially and spiritually accountable to _____.

Between You and God

1. Ask God to reveal His desire for your current financial condition.

2. What step is God leading you to take in the areas of debt, saving, and giving? Journal your thoughts below.
    debt –
    saving –
    giving –

3. What is God asking you to do differently?

4. List below all the different ways God has provided for you during college.

5. Jesus said, "No one can serve two masters . . . God and Money" (Matt. 6:24). What needs to be laid at the cross? Check all that apply.
    [ ] Credit cards
    [ ] A trust in money over God
    [ ] Bad stewardship
    [ ] Jealousy and envy
    [ ] Family or society's influence
    [ ] Not giving or not saving
    [ ] Other _____

6. Now take this list to the Lord in prayer.

God's Will: Right or Left?

God's Will: Right or Left?

The college years are full of seeking. Seeking friends, dates, fun, a degree, but most importantly "the plan." What is God's will for me? What is it that He wants me to do? Personally, I had never given much thought to God's will for my life until I first heard the words major, internship, graduation, and interviews. Like strategically placed mountains along the path of "**my plan**," life all of a sudden seemed complicated. No longer was the ease of high school life to be! For the first time in my life I was faced with decisions that made me ask, "What is my purpose in life? What is **God's plan**?"

Look below at the graph from *USA TODAY* on May 28-31,1999:

Going to a Higher Authority:
What adults would ask a god or supreme being if they could get a direct answer:

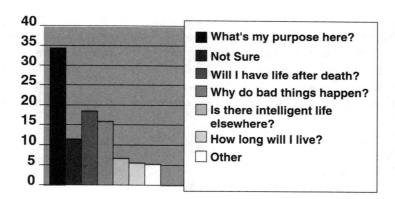

Legend:
- What's my purpose here?
- Not Sure
- Will I have life after death?
- Why do bad things happen?
- Is there intelligent life elsewhere?
- How long will I live?
- Other

If you read the first paragraph and thought, "Man—that's me," well rest easy, because that's the majority! The landslide winner in the *USA Today* poll was, "What is my purpose here?" People around the world (not just college students) have a desire to know God's will. One look at the questions that earned a ranking in the poll, and it's quick to see that people want answers to life. Whether it's healing for the past, hope for the future, or clarity in the present, we each have a desire for purpose.

> "My heart is restless 'til it finds rest in Thee"
> —Augustine

How has your desire to know God's will changed since entering college?
- [ ] Never thought much about it before now.
- [ ] It has become more confusing.
- [ ] I'm searching like never before, but heaven seems quiet.
- [ ] I want to know His will more than anything.

Today's the Day

Sometimes life just looks "greener on the other side." We stare in anticipation of tomorrow as the day we'll seek God, obey Him, or finally find our purpose, when all along God has been waiting for us in the present, waiting for the moment we would open our hearts and let Him work in our life. The time to become a godly man is now!

Read the following verses.
"Now listen, you who say, 'Today or tomorrow we will go to this or that city, spend a year there, carry on business and make money.' Why, you do not even know what will happen tomorrow. What is your life? You are a mist that appears for a little while and then vanishes. Instead, you ought to say, 'If it is the Lord's will, we will live and do this or that'" (Jas. 4:13-15).

It doesn't matter the situation—whether painful or prosperous—if you are not living your life in obedience to God you're not going to discover His will. Obtaining the highest education will be a fantasy. Don't wait for tomorrow. We are only "a mist" that will vanish. Don't sell your soul to a goal or plan when "you don't even know what will happen tomorrow." Make today the day obedience will begin in your life. "If it is the Lord's will, we will live and do this or that." Make a decision to choose the highest education while on campus!

When you make plans for your future do you typically . . .
(Check all that apply)
- [ ] Just think and react – Trust your instincts and feelings
- [ ] Plan and calculate – Trust your intellect and experiences
- [ ] Consult the wisdom of others – Trust friendly advice
- [ ] Pray, study the Word, fast, worship – Trust God for the plan

Three aspects of God's Will

There are three distinct aspects of God's will that provide a blueprint for our lives. Each are unique in the part they play, but all work together in unity. Understanding how God uses each of these in our lives will hopefully provide a clear definition of God's will in your life:

The three aspects of God's will are:

1) **His Revealed Will:** The precepts or moral codes found in His Word.
2) **His Providential Will:** The circumstances He allows in our lives.
3) **His Specific Will:** The daily quest to please Him and find direction for life.

Now before you flip over several pages and go straight to number 3, don't disregard number 1 and number 2. God has a whole lot to teach us before we ever get to **His specific will** for our lives. Winning a battle is great, but winning the war is better. We are going to need every bit of ammunition we can get. Ignoring the facts in numbers 1 and 2 will lead us to make decisions based on feelings instead of faith, and as a result leave us "Missing-In-Action" with God.

His Revealed Will: The precepts or moral codes found in His Word.

This aspect of God's will isn't difficult to discover for your life. His precepts found in the Bible are written in black and white, and often in red. His revealed will is for every person on the earth, no matter your age, race, gender, or nationality. This is God's way of communicating His desires for our life. From Genesis to Revelation, God draws the principles and parameters that will guide us on our journey. The stories and teachings remove the blindfolds from our eyes to see His path.

How do you view the Bible?
[ ] Out of date and out of touch with my generation
[ ] Great piece of fiction
[ ] I agree with most everything it teaches
[ ] It's the complete truth of God for my life

Occasionally, when I'm participating in every male's favorite sport, channel surfing, I'll run across a program called "Behind the Music" on VH1. In a chronological biography, the show highlights different rock bands and "where they are now." Each bio has a typical story line that usually sounds like this: "We were nobodies. We signed a record deal and became somebodies. The money rolled in so we did a lot of drugs. Then a fight and/or a car accident broke up the band. And now we are nobodies again and broke." The recurrent theme of these bands allows us to learn from someone else's mistakes and not our own.

Did you know?
The Bible was:

• Written by over 40 different authors
• Written in two main languages: Hebrew and Greek
• Written over a 1,600 year period
• Inspired by God (2 Tim. 3:16)
• Writers included kings, peasants, poets, statesmen, scholars, and fishermen

— Gordon Thiessen, *Cross Training Manual* **p. 117-118**

The same is true in the Bible. Over and over, we get to witness the consequences of breaking or keeping God's precepts. Take for example these highs and lows:

- Want to know the result of a one-night stand? Ask David. (Ps. 51)

- The benefit of ripping off God? Check the tombstones of Ananias and his wife Sapphira. (Acts 5)

- The joy of laying down your plans for His? Paul has a thought or two. (Phil. 3)

- Wonder what will happen when you turn your prodigal heart back to the Father? He's lacing up His running shoes right now. (Luke 15:20)

The biographies of the Bible let us see the result of decisions in others' lives before we have to make them in our own. It seems so easy to read and learn because it's right there before our eyes. So, how do we miss it? Very simply: the Bible isn't always right before our eyes. It's typically on our bookshelf.

Look at Acts 17:11. Paul and Silas stop in a town called Berea.

- How often does it say the Bereans read the Bible?

- What was their attitude in searching the Scriptures?

Read Hebrews 4:12. What does it say God's Word is for us?

God's Word has the answers to our questions, but we have to commit some time to seeking what it says. It's anything but routine; but it's a routine that all of us need. A specific time during our day when, for no other reason, the world stops for fellowship with God. Creating the habit of listening to the words of God gives a power source for the choices we make. The first step in the will of God is finding who He is, what He loves, and what He has to say about the issues facing our lives. Only then do we plug into God's will and let go of our own.

the highest education:
becoming a godly man

Why do we need to plug into God's revealed will as seekers to become godly men? Take a look at the following issues that face the college man and see what the Bible has to say about them.

- **Cutting someone down, foul language, or coarse joking**
  "Do not let any unwholesome talk come out of your mouths, but only what is helpful for building others up according to their needs, that it may benefit those who listen" (Eph. 4:29).

- **Quitting going to church**
  "Let us not give up meeting together, as some are in the habit of doing, but let us encourage one another—and all the more as you see the Day approaching" (Heb. 10:25).

- **Telling lies or half-truths**
  "You shall not give false testimony against your neighbor" (Ex. 20:16).

- **Messing around on a date**
  "It is God's will that you should be sanctified: that you should avoid sexual immorality" (1 Thess. 4:3).

- **Being self-centered**
  "Do nothing out of selfish ambition or vain conceit, but in humility consider others better than yourselves" (Phil. 2:3).

- **Getting drunk**
  "Do not get drunk on wine, which leads to debauchery. Instead, be filled with the Spirit" (Eph. 5:18).

- **Dating a non-Christian**
  "Do not be yoked together with unbelievers. For what do righteousness and wickedness have in common?" (2 Cor. 6:14).

The formula for discovering God's revealed will is simple:
Reading the Bible = Discovering His Revealed Will!

> "Find a Bible that's falling apart and you're sure to find a person who's not."
> —D.L. Moody

If the Bible is left on the shelf, then so is this aspect of His will. Do you want to know if she's the one? Do you need help finding the right major? Do you need a plan for paying off your student loan? Don't look any farther than the Word of God. The answers have been there since Y0K! Like a wide receiver who always runs his pattern out of bounds or a golfer who hits to the wrong fairway, we must first learn our parameters before we can play the game right. God's preceptive will works in much the same way. Knowing the will of God first and foremost means making an effort to know the parameters of God. Are you willing to sacrifice your time to learn God's parameters?

Which best explains you and the Bible?
[ ] I know I should read the Word but I don't. Thanks for the guilt trip.
[ ] I'm in the Pages only at Bible study or church.
[ ] I go in spurts. Some weeks are good and others aren't.
[ ] A few days are missed, but overall I'm consistent.
[ ] Couldn't do without it and can't get enough of it!

On a scale of 1 to 10 . . .
Circle where you fall in knowing God's revealed will.

1   2   3   4   5   6   7   8   9   10

If your score is low, when is a time that you can set aside each day to spend in the Word of God? Find the time! Be true to your commitment each day.

His Providential Will: The circumstances He allows in our lives.

The providence of God is a comforting mystery, and it's beyond anyone's human intellect to explain exactly how or why things happen the way they do. One glimpse at a public school shooting, a plane crash, or a family illness and you are probably like me . . . dumbfounded with questions and sorrow. It's this mystery that leads us to understand two aspects of God's providence in our lives:
1) We don't know why certain things happen, but we do know He is in control.
2) Providential circumstances are out of our control whether we like it or not.

It's a fact that in our lives God is going to allow challenges and opportunities to intersect our day without ever asking for our advice or consent. Some circumstances will be incredible and you'll love every minute, while others will drop you to your knees wondering why. The choice we as godly men must make on a daily basis is to trust that God will see us through no matter the length of our trial. The story of Job is the classic example of handling whatever comes.

Read Job 1:13-22.
Make a list below of all Job lost that day.

- _____ and donkeys
- sheep and _____
- _____
- _____ and daughters

And you thought you had a tough day!

Two tests and a paper due dim in comparison to the extent of Job's loss. Job knew God was still in complete control even though the situation screamed the opposite. Job didn't abandon his faith when the going got tough. He understood that providence was out of his hands and beyond explanation. In fact, his response is contrary to how most of us would feel in that circumstance.

Take a look at Job's response:
"Then he fell to the ground in worship and said . . . 'The Lord gave and the Lord has taken away; may the name of the Lord be praised.' In all this, Job did not sin by charging God with wrongdoing" (Job 1:20-22).

The faith of Job is, without question, amazing! It teaches us to follow God even when His providence in our life and our own earthly prosperity are on opposite ends of the spectrum. Hear this: Hard times can be as much the will of God as the good times. It's in those circumstances that He chisels us into the image of Christ. Tough days are going to bring us humbly to our knees. The real test begins when great hardship, struggle, grief or pain challenges our life. It is true His will is more about our holiness than our happiness, but providence isn't always bad news. Let's finish the story of Job's trial. Take a look at these verses from the last chapter of his book.

"Then Job replied to the Lord: I know that you can do all things; no plan of yours can be thwarted" (Job 42:1,2).

"After Job had prayed for his friends, the Lord made him prosperous again and gave him twice as much as he had before" (Job 42:10).

His will is more about our holiness than our happiness.

"If God sends us on stony paths, He provides strong shoes."
Corrie Ten Boom
Missionary to China
www.speaktheword.com

71

God blessed Him abundantly for his faith. God's providential will for your life might be full of blessing. It could be as small as a grade on a test or a safe trip in your car. Or it could be as great as bumping into the girl of your dreams at a hamburger cookout (that's how I met my wife) or meeting the CEO of a company who's hiring the day before your graduation. These aren't accidents, but gifts of abundance for your life. Thank Him "for the plan that can't be thwarted" in your life.

Regardless of whether the providence is Job 1 or Job 42 style, two things must be learned if we are going to live in the will of God:

    1. God is in control.
    2. I must continue to trust His heart when I can't see His hand.

His Specific Will: The daily quest to please Him and find direction for life

If you could get an email from God with the specifics about a certain subject, what would it be?

    [ ] What's the plan for my dating?
    [ ] God, did you know graduation is coming? Any thoughts You'd like to share?
    [ ] Should I chose option A _____ or option B _____?
       (Fill in the blanks.)
    [ ] Behind door #2, you'll find your new major!
    [ ] I'm clueless, so any info would be great.
    [ ] Take your pick _____

Destination Disease: Don't stress – TRUST!

I'm convinced that we have made God's specific plan more complex than it truly is. All over your campus students are stressed out trying to find something God is not hiding. Take Paul for example. His ministry was basically to go from town to town. He traveled the Via Egnatia, one of the best highways of the day, stopping at each city and preaching in the synagogue, or by the sea. He didn't have a specific itinerary. He followed God's plan, staying in a town until either he or the local officials decided it was time to move on.

God's will for us is to daily place our trust in His leadership like the apostle Paul did. For men this can be tough because we are result and goal oriented. We are wired up for . . .

    • The destination
    • The bottom line
    • The final score

As a result, the will of God becomes
- A location
- A certain job
- A degree
- A win-at-all-cost attitude
- A dollar amount

The stress of life and pressure of performance mounts as we live a life of destinations, fearing the cost of failure. In our desire for perfection, excellence, or first place, we forget God. We leave His plan in the dust in exchange for our own. The result is that we wake up 1, 5, 10, or 50 years down the road and wonder why our lives don't mean a whole lot! What happened to that education designed to help us be godly men? We finally come to grips with the fact that our drive for destinations has produced a row of trophies and an empty soul. We look at the life in the mirror and see an unrecognizable face staring back at us . . . an accomplished man who has nothing! But is this God's specific will for my life?

God's will is a journey, not a destination!

News flash: **God's will is a journey, not a destination!**

God's will is a journey, but is accomplished in small steps of daily dependence on Him. It's knowing Him and making Him known. It's turning the stress of the destination into a lifetime of trust. Taking each breath, each day of our existence captive to a God who's big enough, strong enough, faithful enough and loving enough to work His plan for us to fruition. It's not copping out on responsibility, doing your job, or aiming high in life. It's understanding that His plan for us is found when we release our life to Him in faith and trust Him.

Journeys in life were meant to be accomplished from point A to point B. God's will is no different. Racing ahead of God just results in pressure or stress. Don't go there. God's plan for you is more about where your heart lies than where your feet take you. It's about your character and integrity. It's about living out God's precepts and loving His people. His specific plan might be showered with all the destinations you desire, but it also may mean the road is steep and the climb tough (remember Job). The key is to walk daily with God so He can accomplish all He has for your life during college, professional occupation, marriage, relationships, ministry and fatherhood.

73

Journey roadblocks that derail godly men . . .

1) We get burned out or stressed out because we live, work, or love in our power.

2) We quit on life for a number of reasons like laziness, doubt, lack of discipline, fear, worry, disobedience, unconfessed sin, lack of accountability, discouragement, guilt, failure, grief, deceit or pride.

3) We measure ourselves by the world's standards, thinking no other person has struggles like we do—so we give up!

4) We get sidetracked by sexual sin, financial immaturity, or the drive for power.

5) We don't keep ourselves in good physical and spiritual condition.

In the garden of Eden, Adam and Eve received God's plan as they dwelt in the garden: Eat from any tree but one. Imagine this: They had the entire forest, the whole orchard, the expanse of the garden, to use for themselves except one tree! It wasn't too much information to process or too many rules to remember. It was a simple plan God had given them. The buffet is yours except one item. Eat all you want and live, or eat of the wrong one and die. Do you see how you can be derailed in your journey to become a godly man?

"Fall in love with Christ and do whatever you want."
—Augustine

We all know what happened to Adam and Eve, but I want you to see an element of God's plan that is still the same today. It's this: All the trees **but one** are there for you and me. Did you catch that? The problem in today's Christianity is we've reversed the equation, thinking God's plan means that we only have one good tree and a garden of bad ones. Therefore we fearfully seek the dot on the map of His will. God's plan is not a needle in a haystack! It's not supposed to be that way. Law school or MBA, do it for Him. Summer internship or camp counselor, know Him and make Him known in that place. His plan is for you to experience the panorama of His grace, not just feasting on one tree, but to eat of many trees. To run, play, work, and smile through a plan designed for your life. Don't sell God short. He has a garden for **you!**

Where the Rubber Meets the Road

Now that we have poured the foundation of the will of God, let's look at four practical steps to positioning your life to discover His plan. Below are four statements with challenging questions that will offer practical positioning of your life.

1) Spend daily time in His Word and in prayer.

Basically, we need to make a daily appointment with God. More than any other entry on our calendar, our time with God is the most essential meeting we could have each day. Without both of these elements, we miss out on the primary way God communicates with us (Bible) and the primary way we communicate with Him (prayer). Time alone with God allows Him to reveal who He is, what He desires from our life, and what He can do through us. It's in this exchange that we form a relationship with God and allow Him to mold and shape us into His image.

What is your prayer time like?

How frequently are you in the Word?

2) Follow His Word and trust His providence.

Following the Word of God is stepping daily in the footprints of God, imitating the wisdom of His teaching and seeking His heart on the issues that impact our lives. Applying His Word allows us to mature spiritually, gain discernment for decision making, receive supernatural power, eliminate a sinful lifestyle, gain knowledge of His plan, take on Christlikeness, and know His will for our lives.

Trusting His providence is taking a giant step—like Peter did in Matthew 14:29-30—out of the boat and onto the water. Though the wind and waves surround us, the question is, "Are the wind and waves inside us?" Peter walked on water for a moment because His eyes were fixed on Christ. He sunk shortly thereafter when fear capsized his heart. Allowing God's providence to steady us is to accept our present circumstances and fix our eyes on Jesus. It's only when we steady our focus that our unanswered prayers, fear of the future, daily frustration, and inevitable heartbreak give us trust in the turbulence of life.

Are you faithful and hard working where He has placed you today? Or are you discontented and always looking to the future?

How has He been preparing you for decisions you have to make?

What does the Bible say on this subject?

3) Be open to His authority in your life.

This is where it gets tough and we become masterful magicians. When His will and our plans don't line up, the art of procrastination and justification reach a new level. We forge ahead in our own direction hoping God will reevaluate His will and change His mind. Being a Christian means releasing our self-proclaimed rights over our own life. It's not our rubber stamp of approval that will get us anywhere of eternal value. It's only when God is allowed authority in our life that we experience true freedom.

Will you do whatever He asks to be a godly man and attain the highest education?

Are you just seeking a "rubber stamp" approval for your agenda or are you seeking His?

4. Step out in faith, following God's lead.

His will requires steps of faith. When you've sought Him daily as Lord and your decisions line up biblically, submit the resume, try out for the team or ask her out! If it doesn't work out, what did you learn? What new aspect of God did you see? Steps of faith require just that . . . faith. Basically, God doesn't steer parked cars. Step on the gas and **go for it!**

What fears keep you from becoming the godly man and stepping out in faith? List one or two of them below.

1.
2.

What does "going for it in His strength" mean in this situation?

1.
2.

The application of these four principles will keep you on course for your life as a whole. The following verse puts it best:

"Trust in the Lord with all your heart and lean not on your own understanding; in all your ways acknowledge him, and he will make your paths straight" (Prov. 3:5,6).

Remember God's will is not a destination but a journey. These four principles will keep you walking His path as you discover more of Him all the way. God's will is a challenging lifelong process. It is not reserved only for spiritual superheros but for His children. In the next week keep an eye out for all three aspects of His will and don't hesitate to obey as He leads you a step deeper into His heart.

the highest education:
becoming a godly man

Encourage Your Group

1. Discuss: If you could ask God one question about His will, what would it be?

2. Ask: Why doesn't God just tell us His plan for the next 60 years?

3. Identify which aspect of His will—revealed, providential, or specific plan—mentioned in this chapter challenged you the most? Why?

4. What's the big deal about living out His will? Why is it so important for a godly man to do this?

Between You and God

1. List three times He has led you in the past.
    1.
    2.
    3.

2. Identify with God ways you are afraid of His will for your life.

3. How does reading this book excite you about God's will?

4. What is hindering the accomplishment of God's will in your life? Share this with God, in confession.

5. Journal your thoughts or prayers below.

Time: Squeezing 27 Hours into 24

Time: Squeezing 27 Hours into 24

Have you ever stopped for a moment in the student center of your college and watched other students? A typical day at most colleges would probably look something like this: In one door and out the other they go, students from all corners of campus. Some coming to eat. Some coming to mingle. Some coming to study. Most, though, are not there to stay long. For most, this is simply a brief moment of hellos and good-byes, and then like the wind they're gone.

Where does time go? Have you ever thought long and hard about that question? Think for a moment—how did my life get so fast? This class to that class, this function and that organization, football games, exams and research papers, and on top of that working to pay the rent. It's crazy! How can I ever find time to pursue being a godly man?

Complete this informal survey on time spent as a college student.

1. I wish I had more time to _____.

2. My biggest time waster is _____.

3. I usually . . .

    a) have too much time in the day to accomplish what needs to be done.

    b) don't have enough time in the day to accomplish what needs to be done.

See if your answers look like this:

1. I wish I had more time to spend with my friends, get caught up on my studying, sit and relax without feeling guilty.

2. My biggest time waster is worry, TV, e-mail, Sega and all the other little distractions.

3. I usually don't have enough time in the day to accomplish what needs to be done.

The World's Most Precious Commodity

Time is a precious commodity! From the college man to the business man, from those seeking to be godly to those not caring, requirements on our time never let up. In fact, when you think of some of the most coveted treasures man desires like money, fame, intellectual ability, and the opposite sex, none are as fleeting as time. In fact, at most junctures in life all of these can be attained or regained—except time! Time is slipping through our fingers as you and I converse. As you flip the page, the seconds are pouring through the hourglass of your existence. Our past is just that . . . past.

Take a moment and rate the following list from 1 to 6, with 6 being the most precious commodity in our society today, in your opinion.

___ Money

___ Intellect

___ Fame

___ Time

___ Looks

___ Possessions

Who's the Owner?

Like most other high school seniors, I was gearing up for the senior prom. Like all the other guys, I had a "hot date." I was dressed in my rental tuxedo, and out on the town we went. One thing set me apart from the other guys, though—my dad's 300 ZX! Under considerable begging and pleading with my father and elaborating on the care and concern I would give his car, he said yes. Off I went, burning rubber around every corner—not because it was cool, but because I had limited experience driving a stick. I was "the man," even if it was only for a day! Friend by friend congratulated me on my car, asking if it was a graduation present. I wish I could have screamed YES, but I had to suck it up and say, "I'm not the owner. My father is."

Like the 300 ZX, the ownership of time is not in question. It's when we realize that God owns every last second of our lives (24-7-365) that the clock on our wall and the calendar in our backpack become His! We don't become the CEO, head-honcho, or boss of time because God has granted it to us. We are simply caretakers of the gift of time. We borrow it from God; we are not stealing it. Likewise, the seasons of life that God gives you, such as college, a dating relationship, or a future occupation are not for sale. God's property has no price tag. We can't claim it, and we don't own it. The Father does! He gives it to all of us.

Have you ever had a situation similar to the 300ZX story in which you borrowed something valuable? Describe it below.

How would your life be different if you realized you were just "borrowing time" from God?

Wristwatch on our Arm and Eternity in our Hearts: How do the two relate?

List two ways in which you feel these two things relate.
1.
2.

Becoming a good steward of time begins with **one solid principle: Know Jesus.** If you do not know Jesus Christ as Lord and Savior of your life, you will never be a good manager of time. It just won't happen. Why? College is full of term papers, due dates, and all-nighters, and until we meet the One who created the time we live in, we'll always be worried and stressed. All over, college students look for something else to fill the time and as a result never fill their souls. Longing but never gaining, striving but never finishing, fulfillment slowly fades into a "things to do list." Only when eternity is discovered do minutes make sense. Time is His creation and so are we.

The Race is Set

Read Ephesians 2:10.

The Starting Block

In Ephesians 2:10 the apostle Paul says, "We are God's workmanship, created in Christ Jesus." The word "workmanship" in the Greek means "poem." Have you ever written a poem? Whether it was done out of a desire from your heart or in necessity for a class, a poem is an outward expression of an inward passion. It should be an encouragement to you and me that we are God's poem . . . His masterpiece! Your eyes, your smile, your dreams were each on His mind when He breathed life into your lungs. You are a product of the Poet! We are not assembly line models; we are unique and special, shaped and formed by His own hands.

Knowing we are the valued workmanship of God leads us to believe that God values how we spend our time. Take a few minutes and think about what you read from the Bible in Psalms 139:13-18; see how much the Poet loves His poem . . . **you!**

In the space below, write down the verses in Psalms 139:13-18 that make the most impact on you today.

The sound of the gun — "GO!"

The end of Ephesians 2:10 reads, "to do good works, which God prepared in advance for us to do." God has laid out a course for us, a race to be run. From the sound of the gun, we move from spectators to participants in each step of faith. We press on past the fear, the doubt, even our own expectations for life, and God prepares a path for those who trust in Jesus. Taking on Christlikeness, we become runners with one goal . . . "good works."

the highest education:
becoming a godly man

Time is not an issue with God when "good works" are at stake. What matters to God is where you are right now in the race! Like a road under construction, our college years are an easy place to detour in our faith. We pass on the opportunity of Bible study, prayer, witnessing, service or accountability, not because we don't want to do it, but because we feel we don't have time for it.

God has your future in His hands! Our only job is to trust Him. We can't change the course of time, subtract or add parts of the race, or alter the path of our life . . . the race has been set. What we can do, though, is choose how we'll run the race—for His glory or our own.

Read Hebrews 12:1-2.

Imagine your life as a race God has marked out for you:
- When did you move from spectator to participator in the race?
- Out of your faith in Jesus, what are some "good works" that have occurred, both past and present?
- In what ways do you need to fix your eyes on Jesus to remain on course?

Run the Right Race

If the course is marked out and the race is set, why don't we have enough time? **We do!** There is always enough time to do the will of God.

Flip through the Gospels and **find one time when Jesus was panicked or stressed out.** You can't. Why? Because He understood the race He was running. Regardless of the situation, Jesus remained unshaken. Whether it was the death of Lazarus in John 11 or the feeding of the 5,000 in Mark 6, Jesus' response was the same. No need to worry. Just trust. In fact, in many places, Jesus was at peace when the world around Him was not. The reason? It was the right race.

If Christ was a student seeking to be a godly man on your campus, what would a typical day look like for Him?

What do you think would be some of His main goals and priorities? List at least three.

1.
2.
3.

Setting Priorities

The most urgent
task is not
always the most
important.
—R. Alec Makenzie
The Time Trap

College students typically manage by crisis and urgency and not priorities. Whatever the most urgent thing is at that time, that's what's going to get done. Instead of facing a busy week with, "What are my priorities?" we often just react to circumstances; we don't plan for them. The typical result is God on the back burner in exchange for our agenda on the front. Setting forth godly priorities will begin to help you discover the good works that God has prepared beforehand. This will assist us in becoming godly men through using the most of every opportunity.

Let's get practical. Use the left-hand column below to prioritize the things in your life, and use the right-hand column to rank the actual amount of time per week you allot for each category. Number 1 through 8 in each column, with number 1 being your top priority:

Priority		Time Given
___	Friends	___
___	Social life	___
___	Academics	___
___	Dating life	___
___	Church	___
___	Relationship with Christ	___

Notice where the discrepancies lie.

Which discrepancy bothers you the most? Why?

Setting priorities can be difficult. The tendency as a college student is to handle whatever is screaming for attention while ignoring those priorities which actually deserve attention. Even if you are striving to be a godly man, this is true for all of us. When our priorities are out of line, our life is quick to follow. The chaos begins, stress rages, and things begin to fall through the cracks. Appointments are missed, papers are late, and tomorrow's exam is now today. Knowing this to be true, Jesus laid out the first two priorities in life for us in the book of Matthew.

Look at Matthew 22:36-40.
List the priorities found in this passage:
    1.
    2.

Priority 1: "Love the Lord your God with all your heart and with all your soul and with all your mind" (v. 37).

Our first and foremost priority in life isn't school, a girlfriend, sports, fun, or friends. It is to be head over heals in love with God. Loving Him with every word and deed. Most of us have loving Him with _____ our heart, soul, and mind down pat. The other part of our heart is left to whatever comes along. But, Jesus made it clear. Our first priority and the foundation upon which the remainder of life rests is with Him.

What does it mean to you to love Him with 100 percent
of your time? _____

Loving Him incorporates two things

1. Obedience
John 14:15 says, "If you love me you will obey what I command." Obeying Christ is more than just doing the big Ten that are carved in stone, but desiring to please Him from the depths of your heart. Obedience isn't a problem when He is loved and trusted.

What is an area in which it is difficult for you to obey Christ?

85

2. Faith

"Faith is the evidence of things hoped for and the conviction of things unseen" (Heb. 11:1). Handling time and living by priorities requires faith. In my own life I often want to be in control, calling the shots. Faith is scary and unknown, and honestly leads me down roads I would prefer not to travel, but the destination is always more of God. That is where life is truly lived.

What is an area in which it is easy for you to have faith in Christ?

In what ways do you trust Him in this area of your life?

If our lives are going to have a compass in a whirlwind of busyness, we must give 100 percent of our heart, soul, and mind to Jesus Christ. He is our direction and destination in the race. Only when we live in obedience and walk by faith is our vision cleared and does our future make sense.

Priority 2: "Love your neighbor as yourself" (v. 39).

Priority two is the overflow of priority one. When you consume yourself with Jesus it's a natural result to imitate His character. This attribute of loving others ranks second only to loving Him. So it must not be taken lightly. Simply put: when we are in love with the Father, we can't avoid anyone He has created. Loving people is our mission!

> **"Put first things first and we get second things thrown in: put second things first and we lose both first and second things."**
> **C.S. Lewis**

This is how priority two works. If we are going to love all the students on campus . . . being friendly to the guy at the convenience store, being kind to the cafeteria workers, looking past your roommates' faults and someday putting your wife ahead of yourself, it must overflow from our love for God. It's loving others as Christ would love and giving yourself in service to them.

Why is this priority two for a godly man?

How do you actively love those around you?

Jesus has given us priorities one and two, but what about the rest of life? How do you decide what to put as three, four, five and six? That is between you and God. But I can tell you this, it will require the use of two little words: yes and no. The reason so many guys are overwhelmed in life is because they are trying to do it all.

Does this list remind you of YOU? Circle all which apply!
• Play athletics/intramurals
• Make a 4.0 (or at least a 2.0)
• Work 15 hours a week
• Known as the household Sega champ
• Visit the family

• Involved in an organization
• Have a girlfriend
• Hang out with friends
• Take a weekend road trip
• and the list never ends

Let me make two statements that will help you keep life under control:
1) A godly man can't do it all!
2) Godly choices must be made!

Prioritizing means saying no to one thing in order to say yes to another. No is a hard word to use because we live for activity and being involved. Having a godly calendar that reflects a priority on Jesus means we must learn to apply the word no more often.

SESSION 6

The flip-side of no

Maybe the opposite is true for you, and you should say yes more often. Your actions demonstrate you are not living as a godly man. Let me tell you, you need to say yes to Jesus and get off the couch. Procrastination and relaxation may be more your style than busyness. The challenge for you is overcoming isolation and giving others a chance to know who you are. This may go completely against your nature, but to make an impact on others we must also say yes. Opportunities for fellowship, accountability, and faithful friendship will be missed if we don't. Impacting our neighbor calls us out of our comfort zone and into a challenge. Will we be there to say yes to that challenge?

List two reasons why priorities three, four, five and six won't make sense without one and two.
1.
2.

Do you typically have trouble saying no or yes? [ ] No   [ ] Yes

Why is this a problem? Put an ✗ beside the statements which fit you.
___ I'm a people pleaser.
___ I'm a couch potato.
___ I thrive off busyness.
___ I'm typically an extrovert / introvert. (Circle one)
___ I don't want to miss anything.
___ Saying yes requires me to do something.

Think about how the statements you chose above affect your life.

Write down a couple of areas in which you need to say . . .
Yes   1.
      2.
No   1.
      2.

the flip-side of no

Now that we have established the first two priorities and the importance of yes and no in all that follows, let's put the rest of our life in line. Place the other aspects of life into the following list, i.e. work, activities, school, social life, girlfriend . . .

Priority (We have discussed the first two. You add the others.)
1. Love God
2. Love others
3.
4.
5.
6.

There it is for the world to see. Listing it is easy; living it is hard. Living this out first requires faith and obedience to Christ. Godly men must have the maturity to say yes and no to the things that will help or hinder them to live the list. Now take a moment to write out a prayer for help in living the list.

The Finish Line

Read 1 Corinthians 9:24-27 and answer the following questions:
- What attributes describe a person who would "Run in such a way to get the prize?"
- What is the crown that lasts?
- Would "running aimlessly" or "in strict training" best describe you?
- What disqualifies you from the prize?

There will be sections of the race that seem to never end. It could be a class, a group project, or your college degree plan. It's easy to feel like we're more on a treadmill than in a marathon. Running with no end in sight, we just spin our wheels and go nowhere. It's at this moment we must reclaim the fact that Jesus is in control of time.

Jot down three or four ways you feel you can begin allowing God to be in control of your time.

1.
2.
3.
4.

Finishing strong means we must let go of our destiny. As you finish the race, it's in His hands! Take a look at how Jesus and Paul described finishing the race with strength still in your body:

- "I have brought you glory on earth by completing the work you gave me to do" (John 17:4).

- Paul's goal, 63 AD: "However, I consider my life worth nothing to me, if only I may finish the race and complete the task the Lord Jesus has given me; the task of testifying to the gospel of God's grace" (Acts 20:24).

- Paul's legacy, 67-68 AD: "I have fought the good fight, I have finished the race, I have kept the faith" (2 Tim. 4:7).

Have you ever heard the quote, "Life is more like a marathon than a sprint"? At the starting line there are always thousands of runners waiting to run. Mile by mile for 26.2 miles the road twists and turns leaving most runners in the wake of a few well-trained distance runners. By the final few miles, the race that started with thousands narrows down to two or three.

Faith is the same. There are always many willing to start the race, but only a few godly men finish strong! Why is that?

1) The length of the race – Discouragement sets in for many students when the finish line is beyond sight. Remember Hebrews 11:1, "Faith is the evidence of things hoped for and the conviction of things unseen."

2) Out of shape – Many students expect to be world class, when their preparation (time in the Word, prayer, church, fellowship, accountability, worship) is little to none. The ungodly man will wear out!

3) The elements beat us up – The wind, the hills, the valleys, the bends in the road, the sun, the fog. Like an athlete, we let the elements overcome our faith. Satan knows where we are weak.

4) It's uncomfortable running in front – Being a godly man and a leader on your campus will always equate to some level of loneliness. That's one of the trade-offs of running strong. As a godly man, you take a stand and keep to it. You are a person of integrity.

5) It's hopeless to run from behind – Wrong! In a real marathon maybe so. But as a godly man of faith, the key is finishing the race. Finishing first or last doesn't matter. Eternity is for anyone (fast or slow) who breaks the tape with Jesus.

The great reward for the godly man is that one day the tape will be broken and heaven will be entered. Our days will be endless and priorities will be swallowed in worship. But until that moment, as godly men on the campus, we must be good stewards of the most precious commodity on the planet . . . **time.** Hopefully, our final words will be equal to Paul's, "I HAVE FINISHED THE RACE."

> **The pains of the race – Too many men like the comfort of mediocrity over the pain of excellence. Laziness and worldliness are enemies of faith in God.**

> **Time. It was not given to us to be wasted or to burden us, but to be redeemed for His glory. Hopefully, our final words will be equal to Paul's, "I HAVE FINISHED THE RACE."**

Encourage Your Group

1. Discuss: If you had a month to live, what are the first five things you would do as a godly man on your campus?

2. Evaluate how these things show your priorities to be a godly man to those on the campus who see you every day.

3. Share why you think so many guys on the campus skip priority one (loving God with all our heart, soul and mind) trying to accomplish the rest.

4. Our goal to be a godly man can be broken down into seasons of life or individual races. Your faith during your college days is a section of track. In which part of the race to be a godly man do you need God to take greater control of in your life? Check all which apply.

    [ ] Getting out of the stands (I'm comfortable in the stands.)

    [ ] Getting out of the blocks (I'm scared and fearful over what others might think.)

    [ ] Trusting Him in the first few laps (It's hard to say good-bye to the old crowd, the old me.)

    [ ] Trusting Him in the middle of the race (I've been running a while and don't want to lose the edge.)

    [ ] Trusting Him to the finish line (I want to finish strong in commitment and trust.)

Between You and God

1. Confess to God what steals your daily quiet time with Him.

2. Reflect on some victories in which you have declared Him as priority one and lived it.

3. Ask God to be the owner of your time.

4. Seek God's direction to know how this goal will affect your walk with Christ.

5. You are at the finish of this book. Share with God your desire related to being a godly man on the campus and in your daily walk.

My Diploma, Please!

Congratulations, you broke the tape! But this is not the finish line. It is actually the starting line. Godliness is a lifelong pursuit! You now have some tools to continue running the marathon. Through the pages of this book filling in blanks, searching the Scripture, and seeking the Highest Educator, the Holy Spirit has drawn you closer to Him with each step. I want to encourage you to use the starting block of this book to propel you for His glory through a godly lifestyle. The principles we've discussed in handling our friends, dating, temptation, finances, God's will, and time are fuel for the fire as we burn with a passion for godliness. Go forth! Seek Him daily. Ask Him to sand the rough edges, and focus your vision on Jesus. The world, your campus, and your friends are all in dire need of a godly man. Be that godly man!

"Brothers, I do not consider myself yet to have taken hold of it. But one thing I do: Forgetting what is behind and straining toward what is ahead, I press on toward the goal to win the prize for which God has called me heavenward in Christ Jesus" (Phil. 3:13-14).

CrossSeekers: Discipleship Covenant for a New Generation

by Henry Blackaby and Richard Blackaby

Discover the six CrossSeekers principles brought to life in a user-friendly, practical, story-telling format. This study sets the stage for an exploration of each CrossSeekers Covenant point. Biblical and contemporary examples of promises made, promises kept, and promises broken, along with consequences, bring the biblical truths home to today's college students.

• 9 sessions • Interactive in format • Leader's helps included • $8.95
• ISBN 0-7673-9084-9

CrossSeekers: Transparent Living, Living a Life of Integrity

by Rod Handley

Integrity. Everyone talks about it. God *delights* in it. We *demand* it. But what exactly *is* integrity, and is it important? If you want to be a person of integrity, to live the kind of life Christ modeled—to speak the truth in love, to stand firm in your convictions, to be honest and trustworthy, then *Transparent Living, Living a Life of Integrity* is for you! This study supports the CrossSeekers Covenant principle *integrity.*

• 6 sessions • Leader's guide included • $6.95 • ISBN 0-7673-9296-5

CrossSeekers: Soul Food for Relationships, Developing Christlike Relationships

by J. Keith Miller

Our relationships with other people are key to happiness and success in life. Too often, though, these relationships become stressful and unhealthy. How can we keep them Christlike? J. Keith Miller examines the false personality we create that leaves us feeling lonely, fearful, doubtful. Confronting this constructed personality and dismantling the self-created aspects lead us to authentic living and Christlike relationships. This study supports the CrossSeekers Covenant principle *Christlike relationships.*

• 6 sessions • Leader's guide included • $6.95 • ISBN 0-7673-9426-7

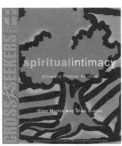

CrossSeekers: Spiritual Intimacy, Drawing Closer to God

by Glen Martin and Dian Ginter

Spiritual Intimacy will intensify the desire of your heart to know God more intimately, help you realize where you are in the process of drawing closer to God, and show you how to move ahead by knowing God on six successive levels. This study supports the CrossSeekers covenant point *spiritual growth.*

• 6 sessions • Interactive in format • Leader's guide included • $6.95 •
ISBN 0-7673-9427-5

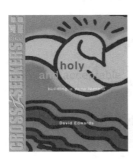

CrossSeekers: Holy and Acceptable, Building a Pure Temple

by Dave Edwards

First Corinthians 6 tells us that our bodies are temples of the Holy Spirit. But what does that mean, and why should we care? This study looks at what it means for us to be God's temple. Through Bible study and contemporary situations, the physical, mental, and spiritual aspects are explored, along with their interrelatedness, as well as what to do when you fail in your pursuit of purity. This study supports the CrossSeekers Covenant principle *purity.*

• 6 sessions • Interactive in format • Leader's guide included • $6.95
• ISBN 0-7673-9428-3

CrossSeekers: Fearless, Sharing an Authentic Witness

by William Fay and Dean Finley
Fearless, Sharing an Authentic Witness equips collegians for sharing their faith with others. Sessions address concepts such as our lives as a living witness (using the CrossSeekers Covenant points for discussion), how Jesus shared with persons He met, learning where God is at work in another person's life, a threat-free and effective method for presenting the gospel, and addressing difficult questions/situations. Based on *Share Jesus Without Fear*, this study supports the CrossSeekers Covenant principle *witness*.
◆ 6 sessions ◆ Interactive in format ◆ Leader's guide included ◆ $6.95 ◆ ISBN 0-7673-9865-3

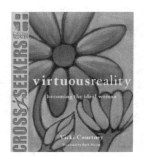

CrossSeekers: Virtuous Reality, Becoming the Ideal Woman

by Vicki Courtney
Virtuous Reality challenges college women to become ideal women as defined by God's standards rather than the world's standards. The primary Bible passage that forms the foundation of the book is Proverbs 31, which describes the virtuous woman as far above rubies. Sessions aim to dispel the world's definition of the ideal woman. They also emphasize the importance for college women to base their worth on Christ, rather than what they do, what they look like, or what others think of them. In this study, college age women will be challenged to pursue wisdom, discern folly, develop a healthy perspective on dating and discover their God-given purpose in life.
◆ 6 sessions ◆ Leader's guide included ◆ $6.95
◆ ISBN 0-6330-0455-3

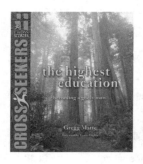

CrossSeekers: The Highest Education, Becoming a Godly Man

by Gregg Matte
Authored by the highly effective collegiate speaker, Gregg Matte, the newest CrossSeekers resource helps guide college men toward a lifestyle of Covenant living by addressing such tough issues as sexual behavior and men's ethics in today's society. *The Highest Education* supports all six CrossSeekers Covenant principles and focuses on the need for accountability as a key for young men to grow into Christian leaders of tomorrow. Each session provides testimonies of godly men found in Scripture, coupled with modern men found on today's college campuses.
◆ 6 sessions ◆ Leader's guide included ◆ $6.95
◆ ISBN 0-6330-0457-X

Transitions: Preparing for College

compiled by Art Herron
For high school juniors and seniors *and their parents*. Practical help for the transition from high school to college—the admissions process, financial aid, loans and scholarships, lifestyle changes, spiritual development, and more!
◆ 6 sessions ◆ Leader's helps included ◆ $7.95
◆ ISBN 0-7673-9082-2